GIVE YOURSELF $OME CREDIT!

A GRADUATE'S GUIDE TO UNDERSTANDING AND ESTABLISHING GOOD CREDIT

JOHN PANZELLA

authorHOUSE®

AuthorHouse™
1663 Liberty Drive
Bloomington, IN 47403
www.authorhouse.com
Phone: 1 (800) 839-8640

Published by AuthorHouse 05/03/2017

ISBN: 978-1-4969-1180-3 (sc)
ISBN: 978-1-4969-1179-7 (hc)
ISBN: 978-1-4969-1175-9 (e)

Library of Congress Control Number: 2014908680

Print information available on the last page.

CONTENTS

I dedicate this book to my wonderful nephews, Nikolas and Marc, for helping me to see life through younger eyes; to my Max, for all the love; and to Marilyn, a kind friend and teacher.

AUTHOR'S NOTE

Thank you for your interest in the third edition of my book, *Give Yourself Some Credit*. Think of this book as an investment in your future—specifically, your financial future as it relates to credit and the role it will play in your life. There's no avoiding it—you and your credit record will be linked for life. You will need credit to finance major purchases such as cars and homes. You will need credit for many other things too, which are covered throughout this book. Credit is an essential part of every adult's life and financial profile. If you are young, credit may not play a big role in your life now but, trust me, it will.

We have a big problem in our society as it relates to credit and youth. Too many young adults do significant damage to their personal credit early in their lives because they don't understand the big picture associated with credit. Damage to personal credit files can take years to correct, and these mistakes can ultimately cost a lot of unnecessary time, stress and money. *An ounce of prevention is worth a pound of cure*, as the saying goes.

Another common mistake I see many young people make is avoiding credit until they need it. Never a good idea – especially when it comes to financing an automobile or purchasing real estate. Not having an established credit record prior to making these types of purchases can result in paying far more than necessary, losing the opportunity to make the purchase, or needing to find someone with good credit who is willing to put their credit at risk and take ultimate responsibility for the loan.

I have not heard of many schools offering focused instruction about credit. General "financial literacy" is taught in some schools that touch upon the subject of credit, which is better than nothing. However, I personally feel credit is too important to lump into a general category. It needs focused and dedicated attention, which is exactly what this book intends to accomplish. *Give Yourself Some Credit* focuses on developing the skills and discipline required to build and manage a strong personal credit profile, and introduces the tools and resources to help accomplish this. It provides the appropriate level of instruction and practical awareness about credit that every high school and college in the United States should offer to all students. Credit is life-impacting information, and good credit management is an important skill that's needed to build a solid, overall financial profile. It's too important to ignore.

I'm a multi-certified credit expert with more than seventeen years of experience in the credit-reporting industry at the time of this book's release. I have traveled all over the country conducting credit-education workshops, and did so for many years. I had the wonderful opportunity to reach thousands of people all over the United States with my message about credit and share all the benefits of having a good, strong credit standing. To this day, I tell people that credit should be treated with the same importance and given the same priority as money because, in life, CREDIT IS MONEY!

In my credit workshops, I covered topics such as how the credit system works, the credit bureaus (who they are and how they obtain and share consumer data), building good credit-management skills, understanding credit scores, consumer rights, explaining collections and much more. It was not uncommon for attendees to want to speak with me after each workshop. People lined up to talk one-on-one about their credit, and they often had personal stories about the credit challenges they faced early in their lives. I heard the same comments time and time again -- *"I wish I knew about credit when I was younger"; "They need to offer credit education sessions of this nature in schools";* and *"Can you talk to my teenagers about credit?"* These comments inspired me to write *Give Yourself Some Credit.* I've written this book with young adults in mind; however, anyone who wants to improve their understanding about credit can benefit from the read.

I would begin my credit education workshops with what I call the "basic building blocks" of credit reporting because to understand some of the complexities associated with credit reporting, it's extremely important to understand the basics. Knowing the basics, as covered in this book, can take you a long way. When I first started conducting my workshops, I assumed most adults understood credit-reporting basics. I was surprised that most did not. But, why would they? Where would they learn this? I started putting more emphasis on credit-reporting basics (the A, B C's and 1, 2, 3's) and I found this approach worked really well. I didn't want to create a room full of credit experts like me. I wanted to create a strong general awareness about credit. If people wanted to learn more, I would point them in the appropriate direction by recommending books, websites and other resources I consider to be reputable, compliant, and objective, which I have also included in this book.

My goal in sharing the information contained in this book is to provide the appropriate amount of material to help you get a good start. I want to increase your awareness about credit and plant some seeds of knowledge into your brain that will eventually serve you well as you navigate through life. My hope is that by reading this book, it will influence some of your decisions, actions, and activities as they relate to your lifelong relationship with credit.

I have two teenage nephews, Nikolas and Marc. I'm writing this book with them in mind. As I write, I'm thinking about them as soon-to-be high school graduates and asking myself the following questions:

- What information would I share about credit at this stage in their lives?
- Why should they care about credit now, as young people?
- What recommendations would I make to help them get started with establishing their credit?
- How should I explain things to them?
- What are the financial benefits of establishing and managing a good credit record?
- What tools are available to help them build, track and improve their credit?

Other credit industry professionals might take a different approach to explaining, describing or defining the concepts contained in this book, and that's okay. My opinions and perspectives are designed to inform and advise a younger generation, like my nephews Nikolas and Marc, about the importance of establishing and maintaining good credit. They're based on my seventeen-plus years of experience working in the credit industry and the many words of appreciation and thank you notes from people who attribute their good credit standing to my message.

In this book, you'll find that I focus on the topic of credit cards. I do this because credit cards can easily get people into a lot of financial trouble, especially early in their adult lives. Credit cards can quickly and easily dig someone into a deep financial hole that's difficult and time-consuming to get out of, and I share information about this topic from my personal experience and the experiences of many people I know. This is all too common, and my hope is that by reading this book, it will help you think about the "big picture" when using credit cards and learn how to use them the right way – as a constructive tool to help with building and strengthening your credit.

As I mentioned earlier in the Introduction, the version of *Give Yourself Some Credit* you are reading or listening to now is the *third* edition. In addition to making this "latest and greatest" version more focused on students and young adults, I changed the cover image, added a 21-question "Credit Quiz" and a "12-Month Plan to Building Good Credit" road map at the end of the book. The Credit Quiz is presented to reinforce what you have learned, and the "Building Good Credit" road map is meant to serve as a guide to help you with establishing your personal credit file from the start. My intention with these two enhancements is that they serve as valuable tools to help you succeed with your credit-building goals.

An important point I need to make here is that I'm not an attorney, so I don't give legal advice. Nor am I a certified financial advisor. So, who am I? I am a financially-savvy credit-industry professional with a lot of credit-reporting industry knowledge and real-life practical experience who has helped thousands of people improve their understanding of credit, and wants to help many more.

Thank you, again, for your interest in *Give Yourself Some Credit*. Enjoy the read. Knowledge is power! Victory awaits!

Victory!
Written by John Panzella

Yes, you matter. You have a voice.
You are significant. You have a choice.

The only time this may not be true,
Is when you don't believe in *Y-O-U.*

So, know it. Believe it. Feel it. *Begin*!
That's all you need to *W-I-N.*

INTRODUCTION

THE WEIRD AND WONDERFUL WORLD OF CREDIT!

What if I were to tell you that by reading this book and following the credit tips provided, you will likely save thousands of dollars over your lifetime? Not only will you save lots of money; many more doors can open for you. Companies will be fighting for the opportunity to have *you* as their customer. This gives *you* greater control over your financial destiny and affords *you* a tremendous financial advantage, which will bring more options that will help shape and strengthen your financial future.

Additionally, my hope is that by taking the time to read this book, you can avoid the serious consequences associated with messing up your personal credit file for many years, a very unfortunate and all-too-common mistake so many young adults make—including me. Yes, I made the terrible mistake of charging too much after receiving my first credit card at age eighteen. I wasn't thinking about the long-term effects associated with using the card and carrying high levels of unnecessary debt. I was only thinking about the stuff I could buy now and pay for later, and all the fun I was having. My thinking was *"Why should I spend the cash in my wallet when I can use my credit card?"* This thought got me into deep financial trouble. I knew that I wasn't required to pay the balance in full, so I kept spending and spending and spending. When I got my bill, I paid the minimum amount due on my billing statement—about twenty-five dollars per month. It was almost too easy. I was buying hundreds of dollars of cool things like clothes, shoes, and lots of other trivial stuff I didn't really need, all for twenty-five dollars per month! This made it very easy and painless to spend more. Well, after several months of paying my twenty-five-dollar monthly bill on time, the credit card company increased my spending limit. So, guess what I did? I spent more. After a few months, I started getting offers for more credit cards in the mail, which I accepted and used. I also applied for the latest-and-greatest credit cards in all different colors – silver, gold, blue, black and platinum! Suddenly, I had access to a bunch of money. *I felt like I hit the jackpot! I felt rich!* But, the reality was, it was not my money. It was THEIR money. All of which had to be paid back.

I recall one credit card offer that allowed me to spend $2,000 and have no payments for three months, then pay only $20 per month. That offer seemed too good to be true. How could I refuse? Well, before I knew it, I was in serious debt. I owed more than $15,000 total on several cards. And although at the time I was making minimum payments of about $125 per month combined, I was being charged about $150 a month in interest and finance charges combined. So, without even spending more, the total amount I owed on my credit cards was increasing! Do you know what else eventually increased (again, without spending anything more)? My minimum monthly payments. They started taking a bigger chunk of my small paycheck. I started missing a payment here and there, which resulted in very high late fees and doubling of my minimum monthly payments. It became very difficult to pay my other expenses with this dark cloud of credit card debt looming over my head. I needed to buy a car, which meant I needed insurance. I couldn't get ahead! My credit card debt kept pulling me under. All of my incoming money (my small income) was going towards paying the credit cards in an attempt to keep my head above water. I wanted to save money too, but there was no way that was in my budget. I had to get this credit card debt down! I felt like I was stuck in a hole that was almost impossible to dig out of and, let me tell you, it was nearly impossible to do so.

The bottom line here is that credit cards make it too easy to get into serious financial trouble. To add insult to injury, I was not aware of the long-term damage I was doing to my personal credit file. All of my credit card activity, including the missed payments and the careless overspending, was being tracked and recorded. My credit report was in bad shape, and I had no idea. It reflected that of an irresponsible person who couldn't control his spending and who was careless about his financial obligations. My credit file was a real mess. I paid dearly for this for a long time. To be honest, it was rather embarrassing and very financially stressful. I don't want you to make the same mistakes.

I had to borrow money from my parents to escape from the credit card nightmare I created for myself. I also had to start getting serious about my spending. Here I was trying to be a responsible adult, and I had to ask "mommy and daddy" for help. It took several years to repay my parents, and I'm very fortunate they helped me. Had they not, I might still be making payments to the credit card companies, which means I would have spent thousands of unnecessary dollars in finance charges. Or, I may have filed for bankruptcy. Bankruptcy can hurt a credit standing for ten years.

I ultimately bought the car I needed, and I secured the insurance that was required; however, I paid over $100 per month more than necessary for the car because of the higher interest rate due to my poor credit standing. I also paid more for my car insurance because of my bad credit. Plus, I had to pay the bulk of my insurance premium in advance. I did not qualify for the "preferred customer" monthly easy payment financing options, which would have made it much easier on my wallet. Why not, you ask? Because, according to my credit file, I was a "high-risk" customer. Therefore, the insurance company required more money up-front to compensate for the chance I would not pay them. And they had good reason for their concern as clearly demonstrated by my poor credit history, including my late and missed payments, all documented on my credit report. I had no idea about the damage I was doing to my credit record by not managing my spending.

Credit is a very real and very critical part of your financial future. Without the proper training and understanding of how credit works, you can do both short and long-term damage to your financial well-being.

CONSUMER PROTECTION—EXTENSION OF CREDIT TO UNDERAGE CONSUMERS

The situation I described in the previous section shows how easy it was for me to accumulate unmanageable and sky-high credit card debt at the age of eighteen. Not only was it easy for me to get into trouble, but many others I know have experienced the same situation. In the past, credit card companies would actively solicit their offerings—their cards—to anyone age eighteen and older. And let's face it, when you're a young adult, you typically don't have a lot of income, yet these credit cards provide fast and easy access to money and make it very tempting to spend without too much worry.

In 2009, a federal statute called the Credit CARD (Credit Accountability Responsibility & Disclosure) Act was put into place to give consumers more rights. It also set some guidelines about the way credit card companies conduct their business. There's a lot written about this Act, and I would encourage you to read about it on the Internet. I have referenced a web address later in the book (in the "Helpful Credit-Related Resources" section) if you would like to learn more.

There's an important component of the Credit CARD Act that made me very happy when I read it, which is the part that addresses "extensions of credit to underage consumers." To summarize, it states that extensions of credit may not be issued to a consumer who has not reached the age of twenty-one unless he or she has submitted a written application to the credit card issuer, **and** either has a cosigner (we will address cosigners later in the book) *or* can demonstrate he or she has the independent means (income) to repay the debt.

Therefore, it's more difficult for eighteen-, nineteen-, and twenty-year-olds to obtain credit on their own today because of the Credit CARD Act; however, it's not impossible. They can still get credit cards if the above-stated conditions are met, and they could still get into financial trouble—*as can anyone age twenty-one and older*—if they don't understand how the credit system works and the long-term implications associated with the intentional or unintentional abuse of credit.

Personally, I like the Credit CARD Act. I see it as a good thing, but it's a small piece of the puzzle in terms of understanding credit and protecting yourself. This book provides you with an education, which serves as a much larger piece.

EXTENSION OF CREDIT

The term *extension of credit* refers to a financial organization's decision to take a risk and approve a loan, lease, or credit card in your name. In other words, the organization is taking a chance by extending credit (their money) to you and is counting on you to pay the money back according to the agreed terms and conditions.

Also, throughout the book, there are several terms used to describe "financial organizations." You will see the terms *lender, creditor, bank, credit union, auto dealer,* and *finance company* used to describe the different types of financial organizations that are in the business of "extending credit" to consumers.

"SO, WHAT'S IN IT FOR ME?"

We all want to have a secure financial future. Achieving wealth helps make life a little easier and it will give you many more options. So, how do you go about building wealth? You do so by *earning, investing, and saving*. Keep in mind that wealth isn't all about how much money you earn. A *big* part of building your wealth involves controlling your outgoing cash—how much you're spending. Throughout this book, you will learn how to save lots of money over the course of your lifetime, but not in the traditional sense of depositing money into a savings account. Rather, this book will teach you how to *keep* more of your money—*lots* and *lots* of your money over your lifetime—simply by introducing to you how the credit reporting system works and how this knowledge, when applied, can significantly enhance your financial well-being.

In our economy, *credit is money*. Don't forget this. And one of the wisest investments you can make right now is to educate yourself early in life about how the credit system works. There are things you should know and can do today that will help you build and maintain a good, strong credit standing, which can put you in a much stronger financial position tomorrow. Congratulations, because you're making an important investment in yourself by reading this book!

We are all so different. That's what makes us individuals. We have some things in common with others and, on the flip side, there are also many differences among us. One thing we all have in common is that we're on the same journey—this wonderful adventure called *life*. As a young adult, you are in such a unique place. You are at a starting point. You've got many "clean slates" where, with just a little bit of knowledge and discipline, you can start on a good note and continue a healthy, positive momentum throughout your life. Decisions that you make and actions that you take over the next year or two have the potential to define your long-term path. Not only will your decisions define your path, but they will also define what type of path you're on—either smooth or bumpy. Trust me when I say that the information presented in this book can help make your path so much smoother and provide you with a significant competitive advantage in life and over many people, both young and old, who don't take the time to learn about credit.

"I WON'T NEED CREDIT!"

If you are one of the few people who will always have lots and lots of cash at your disposal at all times, then perhaps you won't need credit. However, if you are like most people in this country, having immediate access to a big chunk of cash could be a challenge. Credit is especially important during times in life when you're ready to make "big ticket" purchases. For example, not many people have thousands of dollars at their disposal to buy a vehicle. On that same note, how many people have the thousands of dollars readily available to finance their education? Maybe you're lucky and your family set-up a generous college fund for you. If so, you're one of the few. Most of you will probably need to secure loans to help with financing your education. What about a home? Houses and condominiums are a lot more expensive than cars and an education. How are you planning to access the hundreds of thousands of dollars needed to buy your first home? Most of you will look to a bank or finance company for a loan. Your credit profile plays a very big part in securing these loans. You will likely need credit at several points throughout life for these and many other times.

"FINE. BUT I'M PLANNING TO STAY AWAY FROM CREDIT CARDS!"

I'll start this section by stating that, despite what you may have heard, credit cards are not bad. The careless and improper *use* of credit cards can cause damage to your credit and get you into financial trouble. That's bad. It's important to understand the difference. If you use credit cards wisely, they can play a positive role in helping build your credit and grow a stronger financial profile. You may have heard horror stories about credit cards and how they got people into a lot of financial trouble. I shared my story earlier. I realize now that it was not the credit cards that hurt me, it was my lack of understanding and my absence of discipline. I didn't use my credit cards; I abused them. It's critical that if you carry and use credit cards, you respect them, use them with care, and understand how they can influence your overall financial well-being.

In addition to educations, cars, and homes, there are many other "big ticket purchases" (also called "expensive life events") that you will undoubtedly encounter in your life. To name a few:

- Auto repair and maintenance
- Health issues/emergency room visits (with or without insurance)
- Travel—either planned or unexpected
- The purchase of appliances, televisions, and furniture
- Dental emergencies
- Home improvements and repairs—furnace, broken pipes, roof replacement, etc.
- Childcare
- Pet emergencies

I'm sure you can think of a few others. You may not have the cash available when these unexpected events occur, so you may need to use a credit card to cover the costs associated with these and other expenses. A credit card will allow you to pay over time, which could be easier for your budget and overall financial stability. Let's face it – you may not have all the cash on-hand when your car breaks down. Or, maybe you do but paying the mechanic might wipe-out your savings. This is where a credit card can help. It will allow you the opportunity to make monthly payments until the balance is paid. In the meantime, the payee (your mechanic) is paid in full by the credit card company. Essentially, your credit card company is fronting you the money.

To continue with this thought, there are reasons why it's often better to use credit rather than cash to pay for major purchases. First, you can usually get better deals when making purchases online. Many online retailers will only accept credit as a method of payment. This is also the case with some airlines and ridesharing/taxi services. There are other ways to pay, such as using a debit card, which can impose daily spending limits. However, most online transactions completed today are credit-based transactions. There are some additional benefits to using credit to purchase goods. For example:

- Your credit card company can provide proof of purchase if you lose the receipt and need to make a warranty claim or have the item repaired.
- Some credit card companies offer purchase protection and extended warranty plans.
- No need to have lots of cash on-hand. If you lose cash or if it's stolen, the money may be gone for good. If you lose a credit card, you call the credit card company and suspend it. If it has been stolen and used, your liability should be nothing or very little.
- Some credit card companies offer special programs, such as earning airline miles or cash back.
- Responsible utilization of credit will help you with building a stronger credit history.
- Some credit card companies provide you with free credit scores when they send your monthly bill.

Using credit cards to make some purchases can work in your favor in terms of convenience. And depending on how good your credit standing is, the costs associated with making major purchases can be considerably less. For example, if you have good credit, a creditor may offer you a "no interest for a specific timeframe" deal. And quite often, you can get great deals online versus at a physical store or retailer because there are no sales employees, utilities, insurance, losses from theft, and other business expenses associated with selling goods at a physical location.

Having a major credit card in your name can be a blessing if you're faced with unexpected expenses. It's good to carry credit cards (or at least one major credit card) for this reason alone. But like all blessings, if abused, they can become burdens.

GOOD CREDIT. GOOD CHARACTER. MORE OPPORTUNITIES! MORE OPTIONS!

A good payment history associated with good credit management, as indicated by your credit report, is tangible evidence that you are a reliable and trustworthy consumer. It demonstrates responsibility. It shows you are a person who respects commitment and that you take your financial obligations very seriously. From a lender's perspective, your past loan and credit card management practices are a very strong indicator of how you will manage loans and credit cards (and other financial obligations) in the future. You will have access to far more financial options and opportunities in life with a good credit standing. Companies will be competing for your business by offering you low fees, low-interest rates, and reduced or waived security deposits for their products, services or rentals, which means you will be able to keep more of your money rather than paying more. It's like holding a "golden ticket" as a consumer. You will be entitled to perks and privileges others may not have available to them.

On the other hand, a poor history with managing loans, credit cards and other financial obligations can indicate the opposite. You don't take your financial commitments seriously. A poor history associated with managing your past credit relationships and other financial obligations can raise some valid concerns about doing business with you. This can certainly limit your options and opportunities as they relate to obtaining credit or financing. The companies that might consider extending credit to you will happily charge you *more* money to compensate for the higher risk associated with calling you their customer. They know you won't have many options and will charge you more fees, deposits, and finance charges to compensate for the risk associated with doing business with you. You probably won't get any preferred treatment, nor will you be offered all the available payment options a consumer with a good credit standing would be offered. Having a poor credit history can also result in not being able to buy that car you need. Or, you could lose the opportunity to buy that house in a great neighborhood that's listed way below market value.

CREDIT REPORTS AND CREDIT BUREAUS

WHAT INFORMATION IS CONTAINED ON A TYPICAL CREDIT REPORT?

A credit report contains information about your current and past loan and credit card relationships. It provides detail about your credit and payment history. The information contained on a typical credit report can include:

- Personal information: name, address, social security number, date of birth
- Past and present credit relationships (loans and credit cards)
- Account numbers, loan numbers, creditor and lender names and their contact information
- The date your loans and credit cards were opened (how long you've had credit)
- How much money you owe on loans and credit cards (your balances)
- How much credit you're currently using and have used in the past
- How much credit you have available on your open accounts
- Your minimum monthly payment for each loan and credit card
- Payment history, including on-time and late payments and amounts paid
- Unpaid collections, judgments, unpaid tax liens, and other serious delinquencies (if they exist)
- Inquiries: names of companies (or individuals) that have looked at your credit report in the last twenty-four months

WHAT INFORMATION IS NOT INCLUDED ON A CREDIT REPORT?

The below information is not included on your credit report.

- Race
- Religion
- Education level
- Marital Status
- How much money you have (or do not have) in the bank
- How much money you make (or do not make)
- Bank account information
- Loan or credit card declination indicators
- Assets (things you own)

A lot of people think that bank account (checking and savings) balances and income are part of the credit report. Nope. They're not. Keep in mind, in addition to your credit history, bank account balances, income and your assets are often factors in most credit-extension decisions because they, like your credit history, are part of your overall financial profile. Finance companies will look at your full financial profile – income, assets and credit - when making lending decisions about you. This helps them with evaluating the overall risk associated with approving you. Will you be a high risk for them, or a lower risk? What are the chances you will pay the money back on time and as agreed? If they consider you a high risk, how much extra will they charge you to compensate for the higher risk? The information contained in your credit report helps them understand how you've managed debt. However, information such as income, bank account balances, and other assets don't appear on your credit report because they *do not provide evidence of how you've historically managed your debt with loans and credit cards.*

WHERE DOES MY CREDIT INFORMATION COME FROM?

There are three main credit reporting agencies operating in the United States collecting information about you and your financed transactions. They are Experian, Equifax, and TransUnion. They are independent of each other. In fact, they're competitors. Think of them as big data collectors and data sharers. By data, I mean information about you, your existing and past loan and credit card debt, and how you manage your financial obligations.

The credit bureaus *do not* make loans or issue credit cards. They *are not* banks. They *do not* extend credit to consumers. Rather, they are resources that provide information about consumers (you).

Credit bureaus are often referred to as "consumer reporting agencies." They collect information from a variety of sources, such as financial organizations, merchants, collection agencies, and courts. They also share this information with their customers, who are companies and individuals that use credit to make business decisions about you. These include, but are not limited to, cell phone companies, utility companies, cable and Internet providers, rental car companies, property management companies, landlords, auto dealers, banks, student loan companies, insurance companies, credit card companies, mortgage lenders, government agencies, and employers.

Many of these companies have a "two-way" relationship with one, two, or all three of the credit bureaus. This means they will request information about you and your credit history. In addition, some will also report information about how you manage your loans and credit cards back to the credit bureaus to help them with building their consumer databases. Some lenders and creditors report information about your account management practices to only one bureau. Some report to two bureaus, and others report information about you to all three bureaus. It varies, and you have no control over this. And not only does it vary by credit bureau, the timing as far as *when* information is reported back to the credit bureau(s) can vary too. Information on your credit file(s) can change daily whenever new or updated information is reported to and received by the credit bureau(s).

Not all companies that get information from the credit bureaus report your information back to the credit bureaus. It is a completely voluntary "report back" system. For example, employers might look at your credit information to help them make a hiring decision; they don't report anything about your job performance back to the credit bureaus. Some finance companies may follow a similar model. They may look to the credit bureaus to get credit history information about you, but they may not report information about you (your account information, payments, balances, etc...) back to the credit bureaus.

The three credit bureaus also provide services directly to consumers such as personal credit reports, credit monitoring, identity protection services, and credit education. Their individual websites (provided later in this book) provide more information about each of the three credit bureaus, including the scope of their respective consumer services.

WHY ARE THERE MULTIPLE CREDIT BUREAUS?

The three primary credit bureaus – Experian, Equifax and TransUnion -- have similar business models in terms of their credit-reporting businesses, yet they are different companies. The fact that there are multiple credit bureaus makes it somewhat confusing for consumers. Many consumers assume that if one credit bureau has information about a particular loan or credit card, then all three should have the same information. This is not the case.

Banks, lenders, creditors, finance companies, and collection agencies sometimes report information about your account management practices to one credit bureau, sometimes to two bureaus, and sometimes to all three bureaus. This is based on the nature of the business relationships they have with the credit bureau(s). This "report back" program is strictly voluntary. In other words, they are not required to report your credit history information back to the credit bureaus. You cannot tell a lender or creditor which bureau you want them to report your information to, nor can you instruct them to use one bureau over another when evaluating your credit worthiness. Due to the nature of this multiple credit bureau industry model, most major lenders will look at credit reports from all three credit bureaus when evaluating your credit worthiness, as this provides them with the most accurate and complete picture of your credit history.

The fact that there are three primary credit bureaus that can contain inconsistent information about you can be very confusing, but that's how it is. You do not need to like it, agree with it, or completely understand it. But as long as you're aware of this fact, this will help you as we continue down the path of understanding credit reporting.

HOW DO THE CREDIT BUREAUS KNOW WHO I AM?

The credit bureaus build their consumer databases and match records using your social security number, as well as your full name, date of birth, and address. Some names can be very similar, such as Robert Smith and James Jones. Therefore, they typically use your social security number as the primary means of identifying you, as it's considered the most "unique identifier."

When you apply to do business with a company that uses credit information in their evaluation process, you will probably be asked to complete an application as the first step. Or, the company may request this information from you over the phone, and you will probably be asked for your social security number as part of the application process. Think of your social security number as the "key" that unlocks your credit files, which is the reason you should take every precaution to protect your social security number throughout your life.

You can control who sees your credit, but you do not control the information that gets reported to the credit bureaus. Many companies won't do business without looking at your credit first, so you really don't have a choice but to grant them permission to look at your personal credit report, which means you'll have to share your social security number.

Always make sure you are communicating with a legitimate company or using a secure website when sharing sensitive personal information like your social security number. If you are not sure, get their phone number, research it, and then call them back. Unfortunately, there are a lot of scams and scammers working hard to acquire sensitive consumer data such as social security numbers and credit card numbers. Trust your instinct. Disconnect the call or cancel the transaction if you doubt the legitimacy of a communication.

WHO WILL LOOK AT MY CREDIT REPORT?

Your credit will determine a lot of things throughout your life. Soon, you can expect to do business with some or all of the following:

- Cell phone companies
- Utility companies
- Cable and Internet providers
- Student loan companies
- Rental car companies
- Property management companies
- Landlords
- Auto dealers
- Banks
- Credit Unions
- Insurance companies
- Credit card companies
- Mortgage lenders
- Government licensing authorities
- Government benefit agencies
- Courts
- Employers

What do they have in common? They review your credit report to help make a business decision about YOU. They will use your credit information to help with evaluating and qualifying you. In the case of employers, many are looking at your credit information to help them with making hiring decisions.

You will probably have independent business relationships with several on this list throughout your life. Personally, I have dealt with all of them in my twenty-plus years of adulthood. My dealings with them today are so much easier, less stressful and much less expensive than years ago because, at this stage in my life, I know what it takes to establish and maintain a good, strong credit file. My personal credit report reflects that of someone with good financial character and a high-degree of successful debt management. After many years of struggle and learning about credit the hard way, through trial-and-error, I am now a powerful and desirable consumer with a very good credit report. You can be too with the help of this book, and it won't take you nearly as long as it took me to get to this point. You can do it much sooner once you understand how to do it—and the good news is it's easy to do.

REALLY? EMPLOYERS LOOK AT MY CREDIT REPORT?

It's hard enough to land a good job in today's economy, right? Why make things more difficult for yourself by having a poor or mediocre credit standing? As I mentioned earlier, your credit standing reflects how reliable and responsible you are, how trustworthy you may be, and it reflects your character as it relates to your financial obligations.

More and more employers are looking at their applicants' credit files to help with making their hiring decisions. It's up to you to show any potential employer that you're worthy of that job. And as hard as it is to believe, you can lose a job opportunity or a job promotion by not being responsible with your credit. Having negative marks such as unpaid collection accounts or court judgments on your credit report can potentially jeopardize your chances of landing that perfect job. Of course, this all depends on what, specifically, a potential employer is looking for when reviewing your credit file. This could vary from employer to employer, and the practices and guidelines associated with using credit as an employment screening tool can vary based on location.

CREDIT SCORES

WHAT IS A CREDIT SCORE?

A credit score is a number that reflects your credit standing, much like a grade on a report card. The grade you receive is based on how well you performed in a class. The grade reflects your achievement, which is influenced by your efforts and discipline. The grade is measured against a standard performance model. The same concept applies to your credit score. When a lender orders your credit report, a credit score usually accompanies it. Lenders typically look at your score first because it provides them with a "snapshot" of how good (or bad) your credit file looks. It helps them to measure the "risk" associated with extending credit to you. In other words, how likely are you to repay them according to the agreed terms and conditions? How likely will you make all your payments on time and as agreed?

Credit scores fall within a low-to-high numeric range, and credit score ranges can vary. Most credit scores provide a low number (the minimum score) and a high number (the highest achievable score.) Your credit scores will fall somewhere between these two numbers. This concept is very similar to the numeric grading system in school, where you can achieve a numeric grade in the range from 0 to 100. However, it's important to know that credit score ranges are usually not as simple as the 0 to 100 scale. The low and high numbers can vary depending on the credit scoring model being used. Whenever a credit score is generated, both the credit score and the credit score range should be provided, so it's always clear where your score falls within the range.

A credit score that's higher in the range indicates a good credit history, meaning you have demonstrated care and responsibility with your debt. You have a good track record. Your likelihood of repayment is good. You are a good (low) risk consumer.

On the other hand, a credit score lower in the range usually means the opposite; you may have missed payments, have high balances, or have an unpaid collection or two on your credit file. Your track record is less than stellar, and your likelihood of repayment is questionable. Extending credit to you is riskier and, if you're approved, it will cost you more in fees and finance charges.

Sometimes more than one credit score is generated when your credit report is ordered. For example, if a lender orders reports from all three credit bureaus, your credit reports can contain three scores. Remember— the scores could be different, as the information each credit bureau has on record about you can vary from bureau to bureau.

Credit scores and credit score ranges (low to high) can vary based on the type of score that's generated and can be confusing to the average consumer - especially when comparing scores from multiple sources. Much like pasta, sushi and shoes, credit scores come in many different shapes, sizes, and styles. If you're new to credit and just getting started with establishing a credit file, don't worry so much about your credit score right now. Rather, focus on building a good credit record because a good credit record will always produce a good credit score!

A GOOD CREDIT RECORD WILL ALWAYS PRODUCE A GOOD CREDIT SCORE

There are many different credit scoring models in use. Not all companies use the same credit scoring model when making decisions to extend credit. For example, Mortgage Lender X may not use the same credit scoring model as Auto Dealer Y, who may not use the same credit scoring model as Credit Card Company Z. To add to the confusion, companies that use credit in their decision process may have different criteria associated with what is considered a "good" or "acceptable" credit score. You, as a consumer, have no control over this. However, what you can control is *your personal credit standing.* Therefore, your goal should be to do whatever you can to make sure your credit record is in the best shape possible. Again, a good credit record will always produce a good credit score regardless of the credit scoring model that's being applied to your credit record.

CREDIT SCORE VARIATIONS

If you're shopping around for the best interest rate and talking to different mortgage lenders or auto finance companies, it's important to understand that not all lenders and finance companies use the same scoring model. If a lender orders your credit and tells you that your credit scores are different from what another lender received, don't assume there's a problem. The difference in your credit score number may be a result of something new being reported on your credit file, like an updated balance or recent payment. Keep in mind, your credit record at each credit bureau has the potential to change on a daily basis – depending on what is being reported and when. Or, the discrepancy may be the result of the lenders using different scoring models.

The same concept applies if you ordered your own credit report and credit score on a consumer website, or if you receive your credit scores from your credit card company. The score you receive may be a completely different scoring model than the credit scores some lenders may use. And even if it is the same scoring model, it may be a different version or variation of that scoring model.

Bottom line -- don't stress about variances in your credit scores when shopping around. It's not an uncommon occurrence. Ask a few questions and you should be able to determine the reason for the credit score variance.

BENEFITS OF GOOD CREDIT

WHAT ARE SOME OF THE BENEFITS OF HAVING A GOOD CREDIT STANDING AND A GOOD CREDIT SCORE?

- You can qualify for a lower-cost, lower-interest mortgage - saving you tens of thousands of dollars!
- The cost of borrowing money from financial institutions can be significantly less!
- You can finance expensive, big-ticket merchandise at a much lower cost!
- Down payment requirements on loans may be reduced or waived!
- You will have lower insurance premiums and more attractive payment options!
- Utility companies and cell phone companies may require lower or no deposits for service activation!
- Cable TV and other telecommunication companies may waive your equipment deposit fee!
- You may qualify for lower-interest-rate credit cards offering special programs like cash-back or airline miles!
- You can rent a car without the rental car company holding a chunk of your money as a security deposit!
- You can rent that apartment that is perfect for you!
- You will not jeopardize landing that great job you want so badly!
- Less (or virtually no) rejections from financial institutions!
- And many more!

The manner in which you establish, maintain, and manage your credit relationships will, without question, influence your financial future!

Remember, lenders and other companies often look at other factors in addition to credit, such as income and employment, in their decision-making process. Evaluating your credit report and credit score is one component of their approval process, and often a *significant* component!

HAVING A GOOD CREDIT REPORT AND A GOOD CREDIT SCORE CAN SAVE YOU LOTS OF MONEY

A good credit report will always produce a good credit score. This is evidence of good credit card and loan payment management, which makes you a lower risk to finance companies.

What, exactly, does "low risk" mean to a lender? Well, it means that you are a more reliable and trustworthy consumer based on your history of managing your credit relationships well. You've stuck to your credit agreements in the past and have made all your past payments on time and as agreed. Based on your credit history, the chances of you missing or making late payments is very low. Therefore, financial organizations will offer you better deals, including lower interest rates and finance charges, ultimately letting you keep more of your money.

On the other hand, people with poor credit reports will generally have lower credit scores. Consumers with lower scores are considered "higher risk" usually because the chances of missing payments and making late payments are higher based on past credit card and loan payment history. Lenders and creditors will charge lower-score consumers with higher interest rates and higher finance charges to compensate for the higher risk, ultimately costing them more money.

The next few pages will demonstrate this concept. There's some math involved, so if you have a calculator handy, grab it and let's crunch the numbers together. Keep in mind…

Good Credit History = Higher Credit Score =
Lower Risk Consumer = More Savings

Poor Credit History = Lower Credit Score =
Higher Risk Consumer = Less Savings

No Credit History = No Credit Score = Higher
Risk Consumer = Less Savings

HAVING A GOOD CREDIT HISTORY AND A GOOD CREDIT SCORE CAN SAVE YOU LOTS OF MONEY

Example 1:

One of the first major purchases you will make will probably be an automobile, so let's start with an example of an auto loan. The chart below highlights how much you could pay monthly for a $20,000 auto loan financed over five years and the differences in your monthly payments based on your credit score. Remember, the higher your credit score, the lower the risk, and the lower (better) the interest rate!

Your Score	Your fixed interest rate	Your monthly payment
Higher score	3%	359.37
Mid-range score	8%	405.53
Lower score	15%	475.80

- The difference between the higher score and the mid-range score is a savings of **$46.16** per month.
- The difference between the mid-range score and the lower score is a savings of **$70.27** per month.
- The difference between the higher score and the lower score is a savings of **$116.43** per month.

There are sixty months in five years, so think about this. If the difference between the higher score and the lower score is $116.43 per month and you pay this additional amount for the full five years (sixty months), you're paying an extra $6,985.80 for the same exact car because of your poor credit standing. *That's almost $7,000.* Think about all the other things you can do with that money!

HAVING A GOOD CREDIT HISTORY AND A GOOD CREDIT SCORE CAN SAVE YOU LOTS OF MONEY

Example 2:

Let's look at another one. This time we will use an auto loan of $30,000 financed over five years as the example.

Your Score	Your fixed interest rate	Your monthly payment
Higher score	3%	539.06
Mid-range score	8%	608.29
Lower score	15%	713.70

- The difference between the higher score and the mid-range score is a savings of **$69.23** per month.
- The difference between the mid-range score and the lower score is a savings of **$105.41** per month.
- The difference between the higher score and the lower score is a savings of **$174.64** per month.

With the higher score, your payments over the life of the loan will be $32,346.36 (539.06 x 60).

With the mid-range score, your payments over the life of the loan will be $36,497.40 (608.29 x 60).

With the lower score, your payments over the life of the loan will be $42,822 (713.70 x 60).

1. How much extra will be paid over the life of the loan (sixty months) if I have a mid-range score compared to a higher score? (Answer: $4,151.04)

2. How much extra will be paid over the life of the loan (sixty months) if I have a lower score compared to a higher score? (Answer: $10,475.64)

HAVING A GOOD CREDIT HISTORY AND A GOOD CREDIT SCORE CAN SAVE YOU LOTS OF MONEY

Example 3:

If you think the monthly payment differences in the auto loan examples were significant, let's take a look at another example—a home loan and how the payments could vary. The chart below shows how having a higher credit score can significantly help your monthly budget when financing a home loan of $300,000 over a period of thirty years.

Your Score	Your fixed interest rate	Your monthly payment
Higher score	4%	$1.432.25
Mid-range score	5%	$1,610.46
Lower score	6%	$1,798.65

- The difference between the higher score and the mid-range score is **$178.21** per month.
- The difference between the low score and the mid-range score is **$188.19** per month.
- The difference between the higher score and the lower score is **$366.40** per month.

There are **360 months** in thirty years. Grab that calculator again and let's do some math.

1. How much extra will be paid over the life of the loan if I have a mid-range score compared to a higher score? (Answer: $64,155.60)
2. How much extra will be paid over the life of the loan if I have a lower score compared to a mid-range score? (Answer: $67,748.40)
3. How much extra will be paid over the life of the loan if I have a lower score compared to a higher score? (Answer: $131,904)

HAVING GOOD CREDIT CAN HELP LOWER YOUR INSURANCE PREMIUMS

We try to avoid getting traffic tickets because we know they're not good to have on our driving records. They usually result in expensive and unnecessary fines. They can also negatively impact the price you pay for your insurance.

The same concept applies to having negative marks on your credit file. Negative marks on your credit file can lower your credit rating. Your credit rating is a factor in determining your insurance premiums. Therefore, negative marks on your credit file can increase your insurance premiums.

So, the best way for you to save money on your insurance premiums is to be responsible not only while you're behind the wheel, but with your credit too.

ESTABLISHING YOUR CREDIT

ESTABLISHING YOUR CREDIT -- NOW OR LATER?

Now may be a great time for you to start thinking about how to establish your credit and how to keep it in good standing. I'm going to share information about how to approach this later in the book and a few "first steps" you should take. The point I need to make now is that I see many people new to the world of credit mess-up their credit standing because they simply don't understand how much harm they can do to themselves by excessive spending and carrying high balances (close to or at the credit limit) on credit cards. Missing payments on credit cards and loans, or not paying them on time can also do serious harm and have long-term negative impacts to your credit standing. Also, ignoring or not paying the following items can do harm to your credit standing:

- Cell phone bills
- Contract termination fees
- Insurance premiums
- Utilities such as cable, phone, and electric bills in your name
- Checks that were written and bounced due to insufficient funds
- Overdrawn checking and/or savings accounts
- Citations—moving and non-moving violations
- Federal and/or state income tax
- Rent
- Medical bills and co-payments to medical providers

Although some of these items don't appear on a typical credit report, ignoring any bills that you legally owe can result in unpaid *collections* appearing on your credit report. Unpaid collections are considered *serious delinquencies*. They can potentially remain on your credit report for up to *seven years, even after they're paid in full.* Trust me—you do not want collections on your credit report. They can hurt your credit standing and reflect very negatively on your financial character, not to mention the financial pinch to your wallet.

Unpaid collections can hurt your credit standing for a long time, and it's a sad reality that they're very common. Many young adults, with the best intentions, new to the world of credit start on the wrong foot with a serious delinquency on their credit file because they didn't realize this. Not paying something rightfully and legally owed, and ignoring bills, can result in a negative impact to your credit record with long-term financial consequences.

A LITTLE KNOWLEDGE CAN GO A LONG WAY

Credit cards are often the first method of obtaining and establishing credit for many young adults, and this is where many people make *serious, long-term* mistakes that ultimately hurt them. I see this all the time and hear it from people all over the country. As I shared with you earlier, I ruined my credit when I was younger. How I wish I had known better, but no one advised me. Why didn't they? Because no one in my life understood credit well enough to teach me about credit and to guide me. Instead, I stumbled as I made my way down the trial-and-error path. Even today, I've come to learn that many adults don't know or fully understand credit-reporting concepts very well. How are adults expected to teach something they don't know or do very well? They don't teach credit-reporting and credit-scoring concepts in most schools. Some schools may touch upon this topic in theory, but I've never heard of this type or level of practical instruction in the classroom. My hope is that high schools and colleges all over the country incorporate this important book into their required reading programs, and that parents will encourage their children to read it and participate in the learning process.

I think about how this information about good credit management could help millions of individuals, and how this can translate into positively influencing our overall economy. Young adults need to know about credit earlier in life – around the time they reach age 18. Credit is a vital component of our financial profiles, and far too important to leave unaddressed without proper instruction.

ESTABLISHING A CREDIT RECORD WITH THE CREDIT BUREAUS

Now that you know a little more about how the credit system works, how credit is used, who uses it, and how having a good credit standing can help save you money and serve you well with your finances and potential employment, let's talk about how to build a credit file with the credit bureaus. If you are a young adult reading this, you may not have a credit file yet because, at this stage in your life, you may not have established business relationships with lenders or creditors.

Therefore, if a company that relies on credit in their evaluation process tries to order your credit report, they may get nothing back. To have an established credit file with the credit bureaus, you must make an effort to establish one. It's not an automatic thing that happens.

WHAT HAPPENS WHEN MY CREDIT REPORT IS REQUESTED AND I HAVE NO CREDIT?

They may try to order your credit, but the result will likely return a "No Record Found" message back to the requestor, which is expected. Listen, we've all been there — at square one - and you must start somewhere. It begins with building your credit history. You need a credit history before you can have a credit rating and credit score. Remember, your credit score is based on your credit history and, with some of the credit scoring models, you need six months of active credit history to generate a credit score. When you're new to credit, you may also be considered too new to rate. With no credit history or credit rating, your risk level is not very clear to the company or landlord wanting to do business with you, which can put you in a "high risk" category.

WHAT DOES NOT HELP WITH ESTABLISHING CREDIT

Before we get into how to build a credit report for yourself, let's start with defining the things that typically *do not* help establish credit with the credit bureaus:

- Going to college
- Getting a job
- Getting a paycheck
- Getting a driver's permit
- Getting a driver's license
- Getting a passport
- Having insurance
- Having a cell phone
- Having a social security number *(Remember, this is how you're identified by the credit bureaus. Having a social security number does not mean you have a credit record.)*
- Registering to vote
- Voting
- Enlisting in the armed services
- Buying and using a pre-paid credit card
- Opening a checking or savings account
- Depositing money into a checking or savings account
- Using an ATM (debit) card as a credit card

While all the actions and activities listed are important and can contribute to building a stronger overall financial profile, they do not help with building a credit file with the credit bureaus. They *do not provide* evidence *associated with how you've managed debt.* To build your credit file, you must have and manage debt. How do you obtain debt? You can do so with *credit cards* and *loans.* Therefore, the best way to establish your credit is to incur some (very little) debt and demonstrate that you are responsible enough to manage it well by making payments on time and controlling your spending.

Keep in mind, your credit card debt can be paid in full every month. It is not necessary to carry-over credit card debt month-to-month to demonstrate good credit-management skills. Regular and active use of credit is key – even if it's one small purchase that's paid in full every month.

Credit cards can be *tools* or *weapons* -- depending on how seriously and reasonably you utilize them. They can serve as helpful *tools to* build a strong, healthy credit record. Or, they can serve as destructive *weapons* and cause a great deal of damage to your credit record. Only you can control this.

WHAT ABOUT UTILITY BILLS, CELL PHONE BILLS, AND PAYING RENT?

Utilities

To qualify for utility services such as gas, electric, or water, the utility company may check your credit to determine how "dependable" of a paying customer you will be. They may require a deposit if your credit is not good or if you have little or no credit history. A utility company, much like a credit card company, will send you a regular statement with a dollar amount owed and a due date. Unfortunately, this may not be much help with establishing credit with the credit bureaus, although some utility companies are starting to report payment history to the credit bureaus. Currently, utility company relationships are not the most consistent way to establish credit. The practice of utility companies reporting information to the credit bureaus is currently limited. However, it is important to know that not paying utilities in your name can result in a serious delinquency, such as an unpaid collection, appearing on your credit report, which can hurt your credit rating.

Cell Phone Service

Much like utility companies, cell phone companies may check your credit report before activating your service. However, like utilities, this may not be much help with establishing a credit record at the credit bureaus. And, like utilities, non-payment of any money owed to a cell phone carrier can result in an unpaid collection appearing on your credit report.

Rent

Whether you sign a lease or have a month-to-month agreement, it may not do much help with establishing credit at the credit bureaus. Although some landlords and property-management companies have started reporting rental payments to the credit bureaus, this information is neither widely nor consistently gathered and may not have a significant impact on your credit ratings. As time progresses, rental payments, as well as utility and cell phone payments, may have a more substantial influence in helping to build credit. However, as with utilities and cell phones, not paying rent can result in a collection or possibly a court judgment appearing on your credit report.

To summarize, while utilities, cell phone service and rent may not be a big help with building a credit file at the credit bureaus at this time, they can certainly damage your credit standing and credit scores if they're in your name and not paid.

ON YOUR MARK. GET SET ...

If you're ready for the responsibility, start building your credit now! Of course, you must be of legal age and in a financial position to support this. Don't wait until you need credit to start building credit. I see too many people do this. BIG MISTAKE! Don't wait until you're ready to apply for an auto loan to start building your credit. Without an established credit history, you may not qualify for a loan in your name. The amount of time you've had credit in your name is a factor in your overall credit standing. The longer the history of responsible credit utilization, the better this will serve you in terms of the positive impact to your credit rating. So, the sooner you begin building your credit life, the better it will serve you. Therefore, if you are *ready* and *eligible*, start soon, start slow, start small—and start *responsibly*!

ESTABLISHING A CREDIT FILE WITH THE CREDIT BUREAUS —FIRST STEPS!

Now that you've got some background about credit, let's review how to build your credit record with the credit bureaus. Credit cards and loans are a good way to start. There are a couple of recommended "first steps" you should consider taking before getting started with credit cards and loans.

1. **Check to see if the three credit bureaus have any information about you first!** You never know; there could be information associated with your credit file that may not belong to you. At this point, you should be starting with a clean slate. However, instances of identity mix-up are not uncommon, especially if you have a common name or someone in your family shares the same name as you, such as a Jr and Sr.

   You can check your credit reports at no cost using www. AnnualCreditReport.com. This is a legitimate site that offers you a one-stop portal that will branch you to each credit bureau's site to access your free credit reports. You are entitled to a free credit report from each credit bureau once every twelve months. You can request all three credit reports at the same time, or you can request one credit bureau at a time and space them out throughout the twelve-month period. The first time you access the site, I suggest requesting a report from all three credit bureaus. If there are items on your report that do not belong to you, dispute (challenge) all the items you feel are incorrect or misreported, and you can do this at no cost. The site provides detailed instructions about how to file a dispute. Don't worry so much about your credit score at this time. Use this site to verify that the information they have (or do not have) on file about you is accurate. You'll also find a lot of helpful information about credit reporting, protecting your identity, and other credit-related topics on this site.

2. **Open a checking and/or savings account with a bank or credit union**. It sounds like I'm contradicting myself with this suggestion because I mentioned earlier that opening a bank account doesn't help with establishing credit. Information about your bank accounts, including your balances, are not reported to the credit bureaus because they don't demonstrate evidence of your debt management practices. That is, unless you are hit with overdraft or returned-check fees and do not pay them. In this case, you may end up with a serious delinquency, such as a collection, on your credit file. However, a good way to start establishing credit is with a credit card. When you apply for a credit card, you may be asked if you have any open bank accounts. By answering yes (and this will be verified), you may improve your chances of being approved for a credit card, as having a checking and/or savings account in your name can help with building a stronger overall financial picture about you. Plus, there's never a bad time to start making regular deposits into a savings account to start building your savings.

IF I APPLY FOR A TRADITIONAL CREDIT CARD AND I'M DECLINED BECAUSE I HAVE NO CREDIT HISTORY, WILL THAT HURT ME?

Credit card declinations, as well as declined loans, do not hurt your credit. They are requests for credit relationships that didn't happen. A couple of things to keep in mind if/when this occurs:

The request for your credit report will appear as an "inquiry" on your credit file. If you had no credit record prior to this credit inquiry, you would have a credit record now. This inquiry can help with creating a credit file under your name. Inquiries alone do not help with building a strong credit history.

Be careful with inquiries -- you do not want too many within a short period on your credit record. Before applying for traditional credit cards, do your research. Find out if the credit card issuer requires an established credit history. If so, you may want to keep looking. Or, better yet, start with a secured credit card, which is covered in the next section.

If your credit (or lack thereof) is a factor with being declined for credit, you can request a free copy of your credit report from the company that declined you. While there may not be much to review because there may not be much credit history, it's still a good idea to request the free credit report. You might see the inquiry from the credit card or loan application on your credit report, and probably not much more than that. On the flip side, there may be something else on your report that's not accurate or an identity mix-up that needs to be addressed. Taking advantage of a free credit report offer after being declined is another way to review your credit report to make sure the information the credit bureau(s) have (or do not have) on record about you is accurate.

ESTABLISHING A CREDIT FILE WITH THE CREDIT BUREAUS — CREDIT CARDS

1. **Apply for a "traditional" or "regular" credit card.** This can be difficult, because when you apply for a credit card, the company is going to look at your credit report to determine how well (or poorly) you've managed your past debt to make a "yes" or "no" decision about you. But when you have no credit history, are they likely to issue you a credit card? There's no evidence associated with how you've managed your credit based on your credit history because there's no previous debt for them to review. It could be challenging when applying for credit when you have no credit history. If they do issue you a card, chances are it may be expensive for you at the start because they may consider you a higher-risk consumer based on the fact you have no credit history. In other words, they may charge a higher interest rate to counter the higher risk associated with extending credit to you. Or, they may require a co-applicant (someone with a good, established credit history) to be a named on the credit card. If you have difficulty getting approved for a major credit card as a first card, you may want to consider a retail or gas card. They tend to be a little less strict about acceptability, but they also tend to be more expensive with higher finance charges.

   Warning! Applying for multiple credit cards in a short time span can hurt your credit standing, so start slow here and approach this cautiously and deliberately. I would suggest some other ways to get started with credit (covered in the next couple pages) as a more deliberate approach to avoid multiple inquiries at the start of your credit life.

2. **Apply for a student credit card.** If you are a student, you may want to investigate a student credit card. Student credit cards are made available to students with little or no credit history. Lenders offering them understand that most students are new to credit and will take this into consideration. You can find more information

about student credit cards on the Internet by using your favorite search engine and typing "student credit cards." You should find some familiar and reputable credit card issuers offering student credit cards.

3. **Apply for a secured credit card.** Personally, I really like secured credit cards as a starting point if you're not a student. Even if you are a student, a secured credit card may still be a good starting point. A secured credit card is designed to help consumers establish or boost their credit profiles. They're offered by many financial institutions and credit unions that issue traditional credit cards. Secured credit cards require a cash collateral deposit that guarantees your revolving loan. The deposited amount usually becomes your credit limit. For example, if you deposit $500, you can charge up to $500, although you should *avoid* charging-up to your credit limit, especially when establishing your credit. The $500 is the security deposit associated with this account, thus the name "secured" credit card. Some issuers of secured credit cards may offer a credit limit greater than the amount of your deposit. This can vary.

A secured credit card will be issued in your name that's linked to the security deposit. It will look just like a traditional major credit card. As you use the credit card, the amount charged will be deducted from your deposit. You will be sent a billing statement every month. If you use the credit card, you would be required to make a payment back to the financial institution by a specific date to partially or fully replenish your deposit. Essentially, you are paying yourself back. The good news is that your payments to the financial institution are being reported to the credit bureau(s), and this is helping you with building your credit record at the credit bureaus.

Every financial organization is different in terms of their offerings, structure, and fees so do your homework and make sure you compare apples-to-apples before you decide which secured credit card is right for you. A good place to start is by talking with banks and/or credit unions you know.

MORE ABOUT SECURED CREDIT CARDS

If you are fortunate enough to receive money from parents, friends, and relatives as a graduation gift and you're ready for the responsibility of credit, I would suggest using some of that money—even if it's as little as $200 or $300—to open a low-fee secured credit card. The money is yours and always will be. You charge on the card, the amount you charge is deducted from your balance, and then you pay yourself back. In the meantime, the bank or credit union is reporting information about how you utilize the card, including your payment history, to the credit bureau(s). It's a win-win! Use the secured card for the sole purpose of establishing a credit record with the credit bureaus, and never charge more than thirty percent of your credit limit. For example, if your credit limit is $300, never charge more and carry a balance greater than $100, and pay it down, and on time, every month. In fact, you could charge only one or two items per month even if only a twenty or thirty-dollar purchase. Then, pay the balance in full when you get the bill. In a matter of six to eight months, you will have an established credit history and can apply for any type of credit card you want. Or, the secured credit card issuer may convert the secured credit card to a traditional credit card and refund your initial security deposit. In either circumstance, you should be in a position with your credit to choose which credit card offers suit you best, such as higher-limit cash-back or airline mileage cards. And even then, you want to continue to manage your credit card usage wisely. Regular (monthly) use of credit cards is essential to building credit – even if it's only one small purchase per month. Keep your credit card balances low, and pay them in full when you receive the billing statement.

If you're hit with something unexpected and necessary, like an auto repair bill, and you're forced to charge more than thirty percent of your credit limit, don't stress too much. These things can happen. Try to pay the balance down as quickly as you can, and then focus on maintaining the thirty-percent (or lower) balance-to-credit-limit guideline.

Once you have established sufficient credit and you're ready to close or convert the secured credit card, you can get your prepaid deposit returned. Here's the best part; by *closing or converting the account, you will not be losing your established credit history.* That's right! The credit bureaus keep track of when your account was initially opened, and the "length of credit history" factor in your credit standing will remain tied to the date your account was initially opened.

Before closing any credit card, there are a few things you should consider, which will be addressed later in the book. Hold this thought. We will come back to it.

It's important to make every payment on time, even with a secured credit card. If you miss making your payments by the payment due date, you were probably not ready for the responsibility of a credit card and should consider another secured credit card in the future when you're better prepared for the responsibility.

If you are a parent or guardian reading this, helping a young adult obtain a secured credit card can make a nice graduation gift! They can be a big help in establishing credit. But, be warned, they can also do some damage if the card is not managed properly. It's important to understand the responsibilities, expectations, and obligations associated with all credit cards, including secured credit cards.

SECURED CREDIT CARDS—WHICH CARD IS RIGHT FOR YOU?

Here are a couple of questions to ask issuers of secured credit cards, which can help you with deciding which secured credit card may be best for you.

- What are the fees? (There are always fees with secured credit cards, so you might want to shop around for the best deal.)
- Do you report my credit history to all three credit bureaus? (You're looking for a *yes* answer here.)
- Is there a minimum time period associated with holding my deposit?
- Will you convert my secured credit card to a traditional credit card after a period of time?
- What is that time frame associated with the conversion? Will I get my deposit back once it's converted?
- Will my deposit earn interest? If so, how much?

There are many helpful and legitimate websites that offer additional information about secured credit cards, such as www.creditcards.com and www.bankrate.com. I suggest engaging a financial institution with a good reputation and/or one that is known within your community.

SIX TO EIGHT MONTHS LATER...

Let's say you've got at least six to eight months of active credit history under your belt because of opening a secured credit card, which is typically enough credit history to generate a credit score across all scoring models. Assuming your new credit history is a GOOD credit history, meaning that you've used credit every month (even if it's one small purchase every month), made all payments on time (it's always good to pay it in full every month), you've maintained a low balance, and you have not been aggressive in terms of applying for new credit, you can expect to see a credit score that is a solid mid-range score. A mid-range score is just that – a score somewhere in the middle of a credit score range. For example, using the simple example of the 0 to 100 credit score range, your initial score may start at or close to 50. This number might be higher, but it could also be lower – much lower - especially if your six to eight months of credit history reflects careless and irresponsible use of credit. Being new to credit and having a newly established credit score does not mean that you automatically start at the very bottom of the score range. If the credit history you've established is good, this can help you achieve a better starting credit score that's slightly higher than mid-range. Keep practicing good credit management skills and you will see your credit score continue to increase over time.

BECOMING AN "AUTHORIZED USER" ON ANOTHER PERSON'S CREDIT CARD

Another way of establishing credit with the credit bureaus is for a parent, guardian, or trusted adult to add you to their credit card as an authorized user. Some people in the credit industry call this method "piggy-backing."

Your parent (or the person adding you to their card) is called the "primary" cardholder. They have a credit card in their name that's in good standing. They call the credit card company and request to add you to the account as an authorized user. As an authorized user, the primary cardholder will receive an additional credit card in the mail with your name on it. They may choose to give it to you —or they may not. It's their decision, as it's their card and their account, and only they are responsible for it. However, as an authorized user, this account is now noted on your credit report because the credit information for that account will "carry over" to your credit report. Essentially, you are "piggy-backing" on their account that has an established credit history. Let's assume the account has a good and long credit history and payments have been made on time every month for the last several years. This information will "carry over" to your credit report and—just like that—you have a credit record. Seems too easy, doesn't it?

WHY IS THE AUTHORIZED-USER APPROACH A GOOD OPTION?

Because it establishes credit instantly. However, it does so artificially. In fact, someone who is eighteen years old can immediately have twenty years' worth of credit history if he or she is added as an authorized user to a credit card the primary cardholder has held and used for twenty years. With an established credit history, especially a good credit history, the authorized user may start receiving offers for credit in the mail. Not a bad way to start your relationship with credit, right? Well, there's another side to consider. Read on…

MORE ABOUT THE AUTHORIZED-USER APPROACH

To start, when an authorized-user account appears on a credit file, it's coded as such. This code tells lenders and creditors that the account doesn't really belong to the applicant. Many lenders and creditors are not considering authorized-user credit relationships on credit reports for this reason. They are disqualifying authorized-user accounts when evaluating credit files and taking a closer look at the credit scores on file, because some credit scores can be influenced by authorized-user accounts.

Another important point to consider; let's say you are listed as an authorized user on your parent's account on a credit card, and your parent loses his or her job and misses a payment or two. Well, this is going to reflect badly on their credit report *and now on yours.* This is completely out of your control. Or, let's say you have an argument with your parents and then they decide to remove you as an authorized user. There goes your established credit history. This can hurt you if that's all the credit you have. The primary account holder has all the control. As an authorized user, you have no control over the account and your credit history can be taken from you at any time – based on the primary cardholder's desire.

Also, being listed as an authorized user doesn't necessarily teach you the skills and discipline associated with managing your own credit card. You don't get the bill. You're not in control of the balance. You don't make the monthly payment. The primary cardholder does all of this.

AUTHORIZED USER—YES OR NO?

In my opinion, the best way to establish credit in your name and to learn the skills associated with managing credit is take a more independent approach. For example, apply for a secured credit card in your name with low fees, keeping in mind your credit limit is usually the same as your deposit when you open the secured credit card. Use the card at least once a month, keep your balance low, and pay it off when you get your billing statement. In just a matter of six to eight months, you will have an established credit history, built from the ground-up and on your own. And, unlike the "authorized user" approach, secured credit cards can help you get into the rhythm of receiving monthly statements and paying your balance every month. Remember, managing your credit is a skill you want to focus on developing. A secured credit card is a safe and more effective credit skill-building tool than being added as an authorized user on someone else's account.

SECURED CREDIT CARDS, PREPAID CREDIT CARDS, AND DEBIT (ATM) CARDS

There are lots of plastic spending cards floating around that resemble credit cards. They even have common credit card names and logos. It's important to understand the differences in the types of spending cards, and which cards can help with building your credit and the cards that don't. Here's the scoop:

1. **Secured credit cards** can most definitely help build your credit. Like regular traditional credit cards, they must be used with great discipline and responsibility. Secured cards mirror the process of a traditional (unsecured) credit card in that you receive a monthly statement showing your balance, minimum payment due, due date, information about purchases, and the prior billing period's payment activity. Secured credit cards can be a great set of "training wheels" in terms of understanding how credit works and establishing discipline and credit-management skills, and they can ultimately serve as a "less risky" way to begin your relationship with credit.

2. **Prepaid credit cards** (also gift cards) are spending cards you can purchase at many retail stores. Sure, they may look like a credit card; however, they don't really belong to anybody. In other words, you didn't have to apply for the card and it's not issued in anyone's name. There is no binding, legal contract associated with its use and, unlike credit cards, there are no repayment expectations. Actions and activities associated with the use of the card are not reported to the credit bureaus. Once the dollar amount loaded on a prepaid card is used up, it's done. You can throw it away. Some prepaid cards allow you to reload additional money onto them, but that doesn't help build credit.

3. **Debit (ATM) cards:** Much like prepaid cards, debit cards resemble a credit card. They are usually linked to a bank account—either a checking or savings account. As you use a debit (ATM) card, the amount you spend is deducted from your checking or

savings account balance. And, like that of a prepaid credit card, there are no repayment obligations. You can keep spending and withdrawing until there is nothing left. You can either use a debit (ATM) card as a debit card or as a credit card. In both cases, money is deducted from your bank account. The same result is accomplished when using it as a debit or a credit card—the only main difference is that when you use it as a "debit" card, you typically enter a PIN (personal identification number) during a purchase or cash withdrawal, but when you use it as a credit card, no PIN is required. Either way, using it as a debit card or a credit card, it is not going to help with building credit. Many people are under the misperception that using a debit (ATM) card as a credit card can have an impact to their credit. This is not the case. If there are no monthly bills generated and no repayment requirements, then it will not help build credit.

Remember, just because a spending card looks like a credit card and carries a familiar credit card name and logo, it can be very different depending on the category it falls under. Traditional (unsecured) credit cards, student credit cards, and secured credit cards are three spending card options that can assist with establishing and building your credit, and they can also teach you the discipline and responsibility associated with having and using a credit card in your name.

ESTABLISHING A CREDIT FILE WITH THE CREDIT BUREAUS — LOANS

Another way of building (or enhancing) your credit history is by getting approved for a loan from a financial institution. Like credit cards, loans are legally binding contracts not to be taken lightly. There are many different types of loans that may be available to you, such as auto loans, student loans, home loans, and personal loans. Acquiring a loan without a credit history might be difficult on your own. The lender may require a cosigner on the loan, especially if you do not have an established credit history.

Loans typically fall into two categories: secured loans and unsecured loans. A *secured loan* involves an asset that's used as collateral. Therefore, if you were to default on the loan, the lender has the right to repossess the asset and sell it to help them satisfy the unpaid portion of the loan. Examples of secured loans are home loans and car loans. An *unsecured loan* does not involve an asset. They are riskier for the lender because there is no asset to repossess and sell should you default on the payments. Due to the increased risk associated with unsecured loans, the lender may charge more upfront fees and higher interest rates. Examples of unsecured loans are student loans and personal loans.

Student loans are a very common loan type that are of great interest to many young adults. They are intended to financially assist students looking to continue their education. If you are a student reading this and you're interested in a student loan, your school should be able to provide you with details about student loan programs. There's also lots of information on the Internet. In some cases, you may not need a cosigner or an established credit history. This is not a book about student loans, so I'm not going to get into a lot of detail about them. Just know that they are a type of loan that can help with building your credit history once you start repaying them and, like all loans and credit cards, must be taken very seriously and managed with great care.

COSIGNERS ON LOANS AND CREDIT CARDS

A cosigner is someone with a good credit history and steady income who will take ultimate responsibility for a loan (or credit card) even though the loan (or credit card) is in your name, you receive the bill every month, and you are expected to make the payments. However, it's the cosigner who is taking the risk and accepting financial responsibility for making sure the loan or credit card is paid back according to the agreed and contractual terms and conditions. Both you and your cosigner can benefit from you making payments on time, as this will help both of your credit files. However, both your and your cosigner's credit can be hurt if payments are not made on time. Being a cosigner is a big responsibility. A lot of young adults ask their parents to cosign. That's great if you have parents or other people in your lives who are in a financial position to do so and who are willing to take the risk associated with cosigning.

What happens when payments on a loan or credit card are missed and there's a cosigner involved? Depending on how much is owed and the situation surrounding the late or missed payments, a history of the missed payments, as well as an unpaid collection, could appear on both your and your cosigner's credit reports. To add insult to injury, both your and your cosigner's credit ratings can take a major negative hit that can affect you both for up to seven years. Even if the missed payments are ultimately paid, your credit reports can continue to suffer the consequences. Not good for you. Not good for your cosigner. Not good for your relationship with the cosigner.

Another potential negative consequence associated with having or being a cosigner is that there's often no faster way to hurt or destroy the relationship between you and the other person if things go wrong with the arrangement. Remember, the cosigner is responsible for your loan and is often left holding the bag, yet both credit files will be hurt—yours and theirs. I've seen lots of good relationships go bad because of a cosigner arrangement. And if you watch any of the court TV shows, you will see many people standing in front of a judge suing the other party for monetary damages associated with a cosigning scenario. Unfortunately, this happens too often. Cosigning agreements usually start with good intentions, but they can quickly turn ugly if not taken very seriously. Think long and hard before becoming a cosigner or asking someone to cosign for you. Cosigning is serious business.

CREDIT BUILDER LOANS

Credit Builder Loans are another great way to establish credit independently. They are small loans, made by some banks and credit unions, designed to help consumers establish or boost their credit profiles. Not all financial organizations offer credit builder loans, so you may need to shop around to find a bank or credit union that offers them. Once you're approved for this unique type of loan, the loan amount is usually held in a "locked" savings account. You repay the loan according to the agreed payment terms. As a simple example, let's say you were approved for a credit builder loan in the amount of $500 and the payment terms involve you paying $50 per month for the next 10 months. You will receive a billing statement every month over the ten-month period that will request remittance of the $50 monthly payment on or before a specific payment due date. Once your final payment is made, you now have access to the full $500.

Like secured credit cards, credit builder loans are a safe and smart way to build your credit. Every payment made during that ten-month period should be reported to the credit bureau(s), which is helping you build credit. Personally, I like credit builder loans, and I really like the idea of opening and using a secured credit card while paying on a credit builder loan to boost your credit-building effort. Even if the credit builder loan is small, let's say $300, and your monthly payments are $30 per month for 10 months, it will help build or boost your credit profile. If you can afford to do both, a credit builder loan and a secured credit card, and have the income to support it, then do both. Or, if you do not have the income or funds to do both at the same time, consider starting with a small credit builder loan before getting a secured credit card. After the last payment is made on your credit builder loan, you can use the money received from the credit builder loan and open a secured credit card to continue building your credit. Although, after several months of making your credit builder loan payments on time, you should be able to qualify for a traditional credit card without any problems.

Credit Builder Loans vary in terms of their offerings, loan amounts and payback schedules, so do your homework. When you're talking with banks and credit unions about credit builder loans, ask questions, such as "What are the fees?" and "Do you report my payments to all three credit bureaus?" and "Do you offer secured credit cards in conjunction with credit builder loans"?

BEST PRACTICES FOR YOUR BEST CREDIT RATING!

This section's focus is on making your credit record the absolute best it can be. We know that lenders look at credit scores to help them with their decision-making processes about you. Remember, a good credit record will always produce a good credit score. Having a well-managed credit record and a higher credit score means you will pay less for many things and keep more of your hard-earned money. Now that you're on the path to building your credit, let's review some factors that play a big part in your overall credit health.

1. **Pay all bills and everything you owe on time!**

Pay all your bills on time. Seems almost too simple, right? Well, it is that simple. Paying your financial obligations on time and making all payments as agreed will strengthen your credit standing and increase your credit score.

2. **Never ignore a bill!**

With this said, if something comes up and you're unable to pay (and this better be a serious something, because this is not meant to be taken lightly), call your lender or creditor and let them know what you *can* pay and *when* you *will* pay. This may prevent them from reporting a delinquency to the credit bureaus. No guarantee here! They do not want to hear excuses. In fact, they will not care what you tell them. They want their money. Believe me when I tell you they have heard every excuse in the book. Take responsibility and do the right thing. If you have a payment due date that falls on an inconvenient day of the month, ask if they can change the due date. This is a common request most creditors will accommodate. Also, ask if they offer automated alert services that email or text you several days before your payment is due. These alerts can serve as timely reminders to help you with making your payments on time.

3. **Avoid collections and judgments.**

Unpaid credit card and unpaid loan payments often result in collections appearing on credit reports. This is also the case with unpaid cell phone bills, utility bills, cable or satellite TV bills, parking and moving violation citations, and other things you owe that are not normally a part of your traditional credit file. Even though these items don't typically appear on your credit report, they can get there if they turn into a collection. A collection is a serious delinquency that can damage your credit standing and hurt your credit score. And, in some cases, the collection doesn't go away after it's paid. The balance may be updated to reflect that it has been paid, but some scoring models are not forgiving. Therefore, in some cases, a satisfied paid collection can remain on your credit file for a full seven years.

Judgments can also cause significant damage to your credit file and can remain on your credit file for up to seven years. A judgment is a court-ordered decision that states you owe money. For example, let's say you are driving without proper automobile insurance. You hit another car by accident. You are asked to pay for the damages, but you don't have money so they take you to court. You are found guilty by the court. Even though it was an accident and your actions were unintentional, you're ordered to pay all the damages. However, you are unable to pay the settlement because the amount is very high and you simply don't have the money. A court-ordered judgment is likely to be issued in your name and can appear on your credit report resulting in a major hit to your credit record and quite possibly to your paycheck when they eventually start to garnish your wages. Do the right thing, be responsible, and make smart decisions. Bad decisions, such as driving without insurance, can often lead to significant consequences, as the previous example highlights, that can impact many facets of your life including your credit and your future income.

Judgments, paid or unpaid, can remain on your credit file for several years and, like a collection, it can have a major negative impact on your credit score. If a potential employer looks at your credit report and finds a judgment, it may raise a concern about hiring you. Avoid judgments at all costs.

4. Avoid Tax Liens.

If you work and earn an income, depending on how much you earn and the state where you reside, you may need to file federal and state income taxes. There are some variables associated with this requirement, so be sure to check with your parents, a trusted adult, a financial advisor, a tax professional, or the IRS.gov website. Bottom line, if you owe taxes, you should pay them. Not paying taxes that you owe can result in an unpaid tax lien appearing on your credit report. Unpaid tax liens can hurt your standing for seven years or more.

5. Avoid Vehicle Repossessions.

You purchased or leased a car and can't afford the payments, so you stop paying. In just a matter of time, the finance company will eventually attempt to take legal possession of the vehicle hoping to resell it so they can satisfy some or all the money still owed on the loan. This is an epic fail in terms of destroying your credit standing. Not only will all the missed payments be noted on your credit report; you will also likely see a repossession on your credit file. Like collections, judgments and tax liens, vehicle repossessions (either voluntary or involuntary) can damage your credit record for up to seven years and can significantly lower your credit score.

6. Control Your Spending.

As the saying goes, *"Don't bite off more than you can chew."* You do not want to financially overextend or overburden yourself. You need to manage your spending. This is absolutely critical if you want to be successful with your credit. And, yes, it is tempting because credit cards can make you feel like you have "free money" at your disposal. This is the furthest thing from the truth. Keep your credit card balances low. Pay them *in full* when you receive the statement. If you can't afford it**,** *stop charging. Put the credit card away* and focus on paying the balance down and, eventually, in full. If it's hard to stop charging, destroy the card -- but don't close the account.

If you do carry balances on your credit cards, a good general rule to follow is to keep your balances at or below *thirty* percent of your credit limit. For example, if your credit limit is $900, do not carry a balance more than $300. If you end up charging more than $300, try to pay your balance down to $300 (or less) before your *statement closing date*. The credit card balance, as of the statement closing date, is typically what's reported to the credit bureaus and is used in your credit score calculation. A thirty percent (or lower) credit utilization ratio (which will be covered in the next section) is a good credit-management goal.

7. Keep Your Credit Accounts Open.

Avoid closing your credit card accounts unless you absolutely need to, and make sure you understand the big picture impact associated with doing so. Closing a credit card account will eliminate the available credit associated with that account, which can increase your overall credit utilization ratio. Let me explain:

In the last section, you were introduced to the term *credit utilization ratio*, which is the ratio associated with your balance-to-credit-limit relationship. For example, let's say you carry a credit card with a $5,000 limit and the balance is at $4,000. You are at an *eighty percent* credit utilization ratio for this particular credit card, which is high. *($4,000 divided by $5,000 = .8, which translates to 80%)* The higher the credit utilization ratio – meaning, the closer your balance is to your credit limit -- the more of a negative impact this can have on your credit standing.

Credit card balances are generally reported to the credit bureaus as of your *billing statement closing date.* Keep in mind that your balances, as they appear when they're reported to the credit bureaus, influence the credit utilization ratios that appear on your credit reports.

I am often asked the following question: *"Will closing a credit card hurt my credit score?"* This answer -- it certainly can, because closing an account can affect your overall credit utilization ratio. Your credit utilization ratio is measured on each individual credit card account that is open. It is also measured by taking into consideration all your open credit cards. In other words, all your credit card balances and all your credit limits from all your open credit card accounts are added together to determine your overall total credit utilization ratio.

Let's look at an example of how closing one account can negatively impact your credit. Let's say your credit card profile looks like the next chart. You have three open and active credit card accounts. Two of the three credit cards have an outstanding balance. For the sake of simplicity, let's assume all three credit cards have credit limits of $5,000 each.

	Balance	Credit Limit
Credit Card A	$4,000	$5,000
Credit Card B	$1,000	$5,000
Credit Card C	0	$5,000

- Credit Card A has a credit utilization ratio of 80%. *($4,000 / $5,000 = .8 = 80%)*
- Credit Card B has a credit utilization ratio of 20% *($1,000/ $5,000 = .2 = 20%)*
- Credit Card C has a credit utilization of 0%

Adding all your credit card balances ($4,000 + $1,000 + 0) equals a grand total balance of $5,000.

Adding all your total credit limits ($5,000 + $5,000 + $5,000) equals a grand total credit limit of $15,000.

Therefore, your overall credit utilization ratio is at 33.3% *($5,000 / $15,000 = .33 = 33%)*

Now, let's say you decide to close Credit Card C because you don't use it often. Your credit card profile will now look like this:

	Balance	Credit Limit
Credit Card A	$4,000	$5,000
Credit Card B	$1,000	$5,000

Your credit utilization ratios for Credit Cards A and B, individually, remain the same. But now that Credit Card C is closed, what does that do to your overall credit utilization ratio? Let's see:

Adding all your credit card balances ($4,000 + $1,000) equals a grand total balance of $5,000.

Adding all your total credit limits ($5,000 + $5,000) equals a grand total credit limit of $10,000.

Now, your overall credit utilization ratio is at 50% *($5,000 / $10,000 = .5 = 50%)* which is higher than the 33.3% in the previous example when Credit Card C was open. The increase in the overall credit utilization ratio can have a negative impact to your credit standing. Typically, the more available (unused) credit you have (which equates to a lower credit utilization ratio), the better it is for your credit standing.

Before closing any credit card account, make sure your credit utilization ratios are low on all your open accounts so the impact associated with closing an account is minimal – especially if you are planning to finance a major purchase, such as an auto or a home, in the near future.

As a general rule, you should strive for a 30% or lower credit utilization ratio. 20% is better than 30%. 10% is better than 20%. Also, be mindful about your balances when using credit cards with low credit limits, such as gas, retail, secured and other types of credit cards that may start with a lower credit limit. In these scenarios, even a low balance has the potential to produce a higher credit utilization ratio.

8. Apply for New Credit Only When Needed.

Only apply for credit (either credit cards or loans) when you need to. Sure, saving ten or twenty percent on a purchase is tempting, but did you know that every time you apply for a credit card, a credit inquiry is noted on your credit file? When your credit report is requested for the purpose of issuing a credit card or considering a loan approval, they are "inquiring" about your credit status. These events are noted as "inquiries" on your credit report. In the credit industry, there are two types of inquiries — "hard" and "soft."

Hard inquiries occur when applying for a loan or credit card and can lower your score—usually not by much, but if you apply for a lot of new credit in a relatively short period, this can hurt your credit. There are some rate-shopping allowances to this rule. For example, when shopping around for a mortgage, an automobile, or a student loan, there are usually time periods that will allow for multiple hard inquiries without additional penalty. In other words, your credit rating will not be negatively impacted with multiple inquiry hits when talking with multiple lenders, within a defined time period, when shopping around for the best financing rates. Ask your loan officer about this when applying for a mortgage, automobile loan, or student loan. The allowable rate-shopping time period may vary based on the scoring model used by each lender.

It's important to know that every time you apply for a credit card, a new inquiry will appear on your credit file, which can have a minor negative impact your credit score. Remember, the fewer hard inquiries that appear on your credit report, the better.

On the other hand, a soft inquiry is generated and noted on your credit report when you order your own credit report using www. AnnualCreditReport.com or other legitimate consumer-friendly sites that offer credit reports. Soft inquiries also include inquiries from potential employers. Before someone looks at your credit report, it's always a good idea to ask them how the inquiry will appear on your report—*"Will it be a hard or soft inquiry?"* If they tell you it's a hard inquiry, it's important that you understand how this can potentially impact your credit.

If you're looking to make a major purchase that requires financing (such as a car or home) in the near future, sometimes a one or two-point reduction in your credit scores can impact your qualification and financing rates. Bottom line – don't be overly aggressive when applying for new credit.

9. Get into the Habit of Reviewing Your Credit Report.

The best place to do this on the Internet is www.AnnualCreditReport. com. You are entitled to a free credit report once every twelve months, one credit report from each of the three major credit bureaus. You may choose to get all three at the same time, or you can do one at a time throughout the twelve-month period. Checking your personal credit reports is so important, and most U.S. consumers don't take the time to do this. Knowledge is power, and knowing how your credit report looks is critical. You want to make sure information is being reported correctly, and you also want to be sure that your credit file is not getting mixed with a person who has a similar name or someone in your family with the same name. If you find errors on your credit report, you can dispute (challenge) anything you feel is incorrect that appears on your report. You can do this at no cost and directly with the credit bureaus after ordering your credit reports at www.AnnualCreditReport.com. There are many third-party companies that will gladly dispute items on your credit report for you, but they usually charge a fee for their services. It's important to know that you can dispute items yourself at no cost. The sites www.AnnualCreditReport. com and www.FTC.gov provide helpful information about do-it-yourself consumer credit reporting disputes.

Remember, as a first step in establishing a credit record, it's a good idea to visit www.AnnualCreditReport.com as step one—because the credit bureaus may have started building a credit file for you—or someone they think is you—which may not be accurate. If you discover this to be the case, *dispute the errors*. Checking your own credit report will result in an inquiry appearing on your credit report, but not to worry. This is considered a "soft" inquiry and will have no negative impact to your credit rating or credit score.

10. Length of Credit History Matters

In general, a longer history associated with the "regular and responsible" use of credit will help your credit standing, which is a very good reason to start building and using credit sooner rather than later. Of course, some conditions apply to this rule. You must be of legal age to do so, and you are emotionally and financially responsible for the commitment. If you don't think you're ready or if you do not have a steady source of income, then wait until you are eligible and ready.

The age of your individual credit relationships (the amount of time your accounts have been open and active) is a factor under this category, as is the average age of all your accounts. As you introduce new credit relationships into your credit profile, it can lower the average age of your credit accounts. This is another reason not to be overly aggressive with applying for new credit. Three words to keep in mind about pursuing new credit relationships – "Only When Needed."

The longer the credit history, the better this is for your credit standing. Active utilization, meaning recent and regular use of credit, is another factor under this category and can help with building a stronger credit standing. This is especially important during the early stages of building your credit.

11. Variety

They say that variety is the spice of life. Well, it's also a minor factor in your credit standing. As a newbie to credit, you may not have a lot of variety in your credit file. The term "variety" represents different types of credit relationships – loans and credit cards. Some credit-scoring models like variety and factor this into the credit score. It demonstrates that you, as a consumer, can manage several different types of financial arrangements. Don't worry so much about this factor if you're new to credit and just getting started. You will achieve variety in your credit relationships with time and experience. However, keep in mind, secured credit cards and credit builder loans are great ways to get started with credit. Doing both at the start gives you more "variety" than doing only one.

12. Time and Discipline

Time and discipline are two very important factors in establishing good credit. It doesn't happen overnight, so be patient with yourself and the process. You will get there!

MORE ABOUT CREDIT CARDS

MARKETING AND CREDIT CARDS

Don't be blinded or fooled by the fun, glamour, celebrity, and lightness some credit cards incorporate into their marketing strategies. You've seen the images of fashionable shoppers or the photo-enhanced pictures of sexy people enjoying a fun day on a yacht. These are marketing gimmicks. They want you to feel like the image they're portraying in the ads. Some companies don't even call their credit cards by name. Instead, they refer to them as "reward cards." These companies want you to spend money. They want you to *feel good* while you're spending their money. They want you to *feel good* about incurring more debt. This is how they make money. They make money by charging you finance charges and late fees. You, as a consumer, have no choice but to pay them – especially if you do not pay your balances in full or if you fall behind on your payments.

The more you charge on your card, the more they will want you to spend, so they will often increase your credit limit or send a "special invitation" to save on your next purchase if you use their card, and of course, this offer is "exclusive" to you. Yeah, right. The more you spend, the more you will owe. The more you owe, the higher your balance. The higher your balance, the more difficult it could be to get out of debt. The more debt you incur, the more money they charge you for using their money.

They try to make you think they're doing you a favor by offering you a small minimum payment option to make things easy for you. By making the minimum payment, they are asking for a very small fraction of the total balance owed. They don't want you to think about how much you're spending; rather, they want you to focus on the very small minimum monthly payment that's owed.

But what's really happening here? Let me tell you. They are making a nice return on their dollar by charging you finance charges. The higher your balance, the more finance charges they can charge you. In the meantime, you're digging yourself into a financial hole. You're also on the path of hurting your credit standing.

Credit cards are *serious business.* If you don't manage your spending wisely, it could have very severe financial implications, which can lead to missing payments resulting in delinquencies on your credit report.

Missing just one or two payments can translate into strikes on your credit report that can have negative impacts to your credit standing and credit scores. I wish I had known this when I was younger. It would have saved me years of paying more money for things, certainly more than what was necessary, not to mention all the stress associated with my unmanageable debt. Unfortunately for me, I learned the hard way through trial and error. Fortunately, my friend, you have the advantage of this book to guide you.

Before charging something on your credit card, think about this: You are borrowing money with each credit card purchase you make. And when you borrow money, you must pay it back. Otherwise, there can be some severe consequences. Do you really want to borrow lots of money and have that constant, nagging pressure of debt and payback lingering over your head?

Buyer Beware
Written by John Panzella

It's important to remain wiser,
Than the smartest advertiser.
They're experts at appealing to your inner-most senses.
They'll have you kicking-in doors and jumping over fences,
Convincing you that it's important to *buy,*
With visions and promises hard to deny,
That of a happier and improved existence,
Testing your control and self-resistance,
Creating a need in your life for what they're pitching,
Promising a lifestyle more attractive and enriching.
They say that buying their product saves you money.
Saving by spending? Now, that's really funny.
Come on, consumers! Wake up! Get real!
It's time to recognize their attempts at appeal.
Happiness doesn't come from a store,
And not from a package that arrives at your door.
And not from jewelry or clothing you wear,
Not from products for your skin, face, or hair,
Not from a new car, not from a new phone.
Advertisers will never leave you alone.
Because they're focused on their revenue goals,
Creating dreams and fantasies that speak to your souls.
They know what appeals to both you and me.
They're good at this too. I think you'd agree,
Especially when they use fear as a factor,
Or, a sexy model or popular actor,
Who take their piece of the revenue pie,
As you kiss your hard-earned money goodbye.
They don't care if you can afford it or not.
Their goal is to profit and take what you've got.
So, the next time you experience an urge to spend,
Stand on your own. Don't surrender to trend.

CREDIT CARDS—HELPFUL TIPS TO HELP YOU SUCCEED WITH CREDIT!

- **Paying credit cards on time and (whenever possible) in full!** You should try to pay your credit card balances in full each month. If you need to carry a balance, make sure you pay it down as soon as you can. Remember, the lower your credit utilization ratio on each individual credit card and for all credit cards total, the better this will be for your credit standing. Strive for a credit utilization ratio of 30% or lower! Also, by paying your credit card(s) in full every month, you can avoid finance charges associated with carrying a balance from month-to-month.

- **Ask your credit card company if they offer alert services.** Some credit card companies will text or email you days before your payment is due. And sometimes they will text or email you when purchases are made, which could be a great way to monitor the use of your card to ensure there is no unauthorized activity.

- **Avoid the "Minimum Payment" Mindset!** Most credit cards will give you the option of paying a small minimum payment on your billing statements to help make things easy for you. Rather than focusing on the minimum payment that's due, keep your focus on your total balance. For example, you have a credit card with a balance of $2,500. The minimum payment owed each month is 2.5% of the balance and the interest is at 18%. If you make only the minimum payment each month, it would take you more than 200 months (that's more than 16 years) to pay off the entire balance. In this example, your initial balance of $2500 would cost you more than $3000 in interest alone. Minimum payments should never be your focus.

- **Minimum or Bust!** If you think you can pay less than the minimum due amount and still get the "credit" for making that payment, think again. The credit card company will accept your payment, and the amount you paid will get deducted from your total balance, but the payment will be considered late. Paying less than the minimum amount owed is usually treated like a missed payment and can negatively impact your credit standing. Plus, you may be subject to extra fees associated with missing your minimum required payment.

- **Do not rely on payment "grace periods."** A grace period is a period of time after the payment due date, usually a few days, that allows you to make a payment without your payment being considered late. Pretend grace periods don't exist. Make every effort to make all payments before the payment due date. Grace periods are good in case there are delays in mail delivery, or if your payment due date falls during a three-day holiday weekend when mail service is not in commission. They're nice to have in case you need them, but don't rely on them. Focus on the payment due date and allow ample time for the payment to be received and to post. Creditors typically won't report you to the credit bureaus as late if your payment is received after the due date and within the grace period; however, they may still charge you a late fee for paying after the payment due date.

- **Change the payment due date if it falls on an inconvenient date.** For example, if your regular payment due date is the fifth of the month, but you get paid on the fifteenth, call the credit card company and ask them to move your regular due date to a later day in the month, which should give you ample time to make your regular monthly payments on time.

- **Only charge what you can afford to pay in full when you get the next bill!** As we discussed earlier, sometimes things happen that are costly and unexpected. If you're unable to pay in full, don't stress too hard. Create a plan to pay the balance down as quickly as you can, and suspend all unnecessary spending until your balance is paid in full. Put yourself into "retail lockdown" mode!

- **Control your spending!** There's a catchy phrase that I use whenever I feel like I'm being tempted to buy something based on e-mail offers, magazine ads, and TV commercials. I say to myself, *"I am wiser than the smartest advertiser!"* This works for me. It reminds me that they can't fool me and I'm not going to fall for their flashy, trendy images and blindly buy their products.

There's no need to spend unnecessary money to look or play any part in life. Keep things simple, and less is more!

- **If you're not comfortable using a credit card for incidental spending, then don't.** Use your debit card for your everyday spending. However, you can link auto-payments, such as monthly music or movie-streaming subscription services to your credit card. Or, perhaps your monthly cell phone bill. And, yes, you can do this with a secured credit card. Then, put your credit card away and use cash or your debit card for your incidental expenses. You will receive a monthly credit card bill showing the charges to your card from the auto-payments. Once you receive the credit card bill, pay the balance in full before the payment due date. This is a smart way to build your credit without the risk or temptation associated with carrying a credit card. Remember, don't wait until you need credit (like when you're ready to buy a car) to establish credit. Length of credit history matters!

- **Create a spending budget of your financial obligations and social activities.** Make a list of your fixed expenses (these are expenses that are the same every month) and your variable expenses (these are expenses that can vary month-to-month). Assign a dollar amount to each. Post your budget in a place you see it every day, and *stick to it*!

- **Make sure your budget includes regular deposits into a savings account.** Saving a little bit every week, or at least every month, can turn into a nice little nest egg. Plus, a savings account is always good to have in the event of emergencies.

- **Always be very protective of your credit card numbers.** Don't let store clerks, taxi drivers or anyone else write down your credit card numbers. Always *swipe* your card. If you see someone starting to write your number down, question it!

- **Make sure you know who to call if your credit card is lost or stolen.** Add your credit card customer service numbers to your contact list in your phone (and make sure your phone is password protected). Also, keep the information that was sent with your card in a safe, secure place. Notify the credit card company *immediately* if your card is lost or stolen. They can put an immediate stop on the card and issue a new card with a different account number in your name. Additionally, consider putting a "fraud alert" on your credit files with the credit bureaus. This will let any company looking at your credit report know that there is a chance of fraud and that it may not be you applying for credit. The company looking at your report, before approving a new credit card or loan in your name, must take extra steps to verify it is you, and not an imposter using your name, applying for credit. Go to any of the credit bureau websites and do a search for "fraud alert" to get more information about the different types of fraud alerts.

- **Credit card numbers stored on web sites, smart phone apps, etc.…** If your credit card was lost or stolen and a replacement card with a new account number has been issued, you may need to update your on-line accounts, smart phone and tablet apps with the new credit card number, otherwise your purchases, subscriptions and auto-renewals may not be processed, which can create a disruption in services. This could include highway toll readers, concert and live performance ticket retailers, other on-line retailers, back-up storage providers, online music and media retailers, and auto-payment processes, etc. Keep a record of all the sites and apps that store your credit card information.

- **Verify all charges on your credit card statements.** Make sure there is no unauthorized use occurring. Create an online account that allows you to check your account status and purchases at any time, and only do so over a secured internet connection.

- **Get into the habit of changing your passwords for all your online accounts.** Some online retailers may store your credit card number for fast and convenient checkout when shopping online. You want to make sure your identity, including your financial and other personal information, is always protected by changing your passwords regularly.

- **Always notify your creditors when you change your address.** It's your responsibility to notify lenders and creditors when you move. If you move and you don't notify them, the billing statements may not get to you. Even if you do not receive a bill, you are still under the same obligation as if you received one. In other words, you can still have payments that are owed by a specific due date. The *"I didn't get a bill so I didn't pay"* and *"it got lost in the mail"* excuses don't work.

- **Never use a credit card for a cash advance!** The finance charges combined with the cash advance fees make it a very expensive way to get cash, and it's a fast-track way to get yourself into financial trouble.

- **Be aware of debt collection scams!** You may get a call from a company claiming you owe them money from an old cell phone bill or an old credit card. When in doubt, be sure to get the name of the company calling you and as much information about them and their company as possible. *Never provide them with any personal information!* For more information about fake debt collectors, check-out the site: www.consumer.ftc.gov/articles/0258-fake-debt-collectors

TRAVELING OVERSEAS WITH CREDIT CARDS

Before traveling overseas, be sure to advise your bank and credit card companies of your travel plans. They will likely ask where you're going as well as the dates you will be there. Many credit card companies monitor your normal spending patterns. If they notice something outside of your normal spending pattern, such as a big purchase or charges coming from a country outside of the United States, they will sometimes try to call you to get an authorization before approving the charge. With this in mind, it may be difficult for them to reach you if you're traveling overseas. Let them know, in advance, of your travel plans. This may prevent any unexpected interruptions associated with using your credit cards and/or bank debit ATM card while you travel.

And while you're on the phone with them, be sure to ask for a number you can call if, in the event, you need to reach them while you're traveling outside of the United States. This is a good time to make sure they have your current address and phone number too.

It's a good idea to make two sets of photocopies of your credit cards, passport, driver's license and any other pertinent documents when traveling abroad; both the front and back sides of the documents and cards. Write the bank and credit card contact numbers on the copies. Take one set with you. Keep the copies in a safe place where you won't lose them and where they're secure. Seal the other set in an envelope and leave this set with someone trusted back at home. If you lose everything while you travel, at least you'll have something to work with - and something that can be faxed or scanned and emailed if need be.

You can even take photographs of your documents and cards with your phone. Whatever you decide, make sure you keep this information secure. If you use your cellphone camera, make sure it's password protected and locked. You don't want anyone else accessing this highly confidential information

WARNING: THOUGHTS THAT CAN GET YOU INTO CREDIT TROUBLE!

I managed to get into serious trouble with my credit when I was younger, and I know many other people who did the same thing. I asked friends and family about the credit-related thoughts that got them into credit trouble in their pasts. Here are mine and some of theirs:

"It's only twenty-five dollars per month if I charge it on my credit card. No big deal. I can handle that."

Don't think of your debt or any purchase you make as a monthly payment amount. Keep your focus on the entire balance. Sure, twenty-five dollars per month may not seem like a lot of money, but if your total balance is high, you may be accruing twenty-five dollars or more in finance charges every month. Therefore, if you're making the twenty-five-dollar minimum due payments, your balance could be increasing every month because the amount it's costing you to carry a balance is more than the minimum payment owed. Sounds crazy, doesn't it? Focusing on the minimum payment has gotten a lot of people into big financial trouble

"Money's a little tight this month, so I'll just skip my payment and pay double next month."

Regular on-time payments are a major factor in determining your credit score. If you are experiencing money issues, be sure to call your creditor to work something out with them, but only if you must. This type of request should be used in case of an emergency and should never be the norm. Creditors are under no obligation to accommodate you, although some of them may, especially if you have a good track record with them. Never ignore a bill!

"I paid more than the minimum payment due last month and the month before that, so I'm ahead of the game. So, it's okay if I don't make this month's payment."

Again, regular on-time payments are a major part of your credit health. Don't miss a payment. Make every payment, and always pay on time. Paying more than the minimum due is a good practice. It pays your balance down faster and can help reduce your finance charges, but it doesn't excuse you from making at least the minimum payment due every month a payment is owed.

"No interest for twenty-four months! What a great promotional deal!"

It seems like a great deal, and certainly can be if you make every payment on time and as agreed. If you miss one payment, even if it's the last one, you may be responsible for *all* the interest you *would have* paid under normal financing terms. And you may be subject to a higher finance charge. Be very careful with all promotional offers and be sure to always read the fine print.

"I make all my payments on time and have paid some things in full recently. I don't have to look at my credit report—I know I have a good score. I'm not too worried."

All too often, it's what you don't know that can hurt you. Your credit report may contain an error that might be negatively impacting your credit standing. Perhaps someone may have opened a new credit card account using your social security number. Or, if you have a common name, your credit files may be mixed. You will not know this unless you see it on your credit report. If this occurs, you need to act immediately. Taking an "out of sight, out of mind" approach to your credit reports can be dangerous to your financial standing. Be proactive. Start reviewing your credit reports at least once a year using www.AnnualCreditReport.com to make sure your credit report is accurate. If you find something incorrect, dispute it

"I received my first credit card. I should charge up to my credit limit and pay it down a little bit every month."

Nope. It's never a good idea to max-out a credit card. Doing so uses all your available credit, so there's nothing left for emergencies. And having a maxed-out card implies that you are financially over-extended. You're much better off using the new credit card every month by making a small purchase, and paying it in full after receiving the billing statement. Regular and active use of credit is key to building a strong credit report.

"I should not pay my credit cards in full. I need to carry balances on my credit cards to help optimize my credit standing."

Carrying balances month-to-month on credit cards does not help optimize your credit. This is a common myth. Remember, the credit card balance as of the billing statement closing date is reported to the credit bureaus. After you receive your credit card bill, you could pay it in full. The following month, your new spending activity, last month's payment and the new credit card balance will be reported to the credit bureau(s). This demonstrates regular use and a balance that's reported every month – even when the balance is paid after the statement is generated. There's no benefit associated with carrying a balance on your credit cards month-to-month and not paying your credit cards in full. In fact, doing so will result in paying additional finance charges. Use a credit card regularly (monthly), keep your balance low (as of the statement closing date when it's reported to the credit bureaus), then pay the balance after receiving the bill (and before the payment due date).

"I made some credit mistakes in my past. I'm afraid to look at my credit report."

We're human. We all make mistakes. There's no better time than now to implement a credit improvement plan. This may involve seeking credit counseling. The first step to getting on a better path is to determine where you are now and create a realistic plan to move forward. And the best way to start is by ordering your credit reports using www.AnnualCreditReport.com. The question you need to ask yourself is, *"Where do I want to be a year from now?"* Do you want to be in the same position with your credit or in an improved position? If your answer is *an improved position*, then get started today. Dive in! Do it! Order your report and seek the advice of an experienced non-profit agency, such as the National Foundation for Credit Counseling (www.NFCC.org) that can help. Remember, time and discipline are key factors in any self-improvement plan.

"I just went through a bad break-up. I'm ready to do some serious shopping to cheer myself up."

Be cautious with impulse or rebound purchases. And beware of those deals that are "too good to pass up." We all like nice things, but be sensible with your credit card purchases. One afternoon in the mall can create years of strain to your budget and a lot of damage to your credit standing. You should manage your spending rather than your spending managing you.

"They said I can settle the debt for less than I owe. That's great news!"

Not so fast. While it may seem like a good option, any type of settlement or charge-off applied to unpaid debt can result in a serious delinquency on your credit report. Make sure you understand the big picture associated with debt settlement. The Federal Trade Commission's website (www.FTC.gov) offers comprehensive information about debt settlement.

"I'm not too worried about my credit file and credit score. My fiancée has good credit. Once we're married, that will automatically give my credit a lift."

Credit files belong to individuals. Married couples maintain their own individual credit files at the credit bureaus. You may have joint credit card accounts, or both of your names may be on the same loan. If that's the case, the credit cards you share and any loans containing both of your names will appear on both of your individual credit reports. However, don't think because you're getting married your credit files get merged. Not the case.

"I really can't afford this, but ..."

If you can't afford it and you don't need it, then don't buy it. It's that simple.

CREDIT MISHAPS – NOW WHAT?

BE KIND TO YOURSELF

You've made a few mistakes with your credit. Maybe you missed a payment or two. Maybe you've spent too much and your balances are too high and a bit out of control. Or, maybe you've got a couple of unpaid collections on your credit file. Or, maybe you have a judgment. We are human. We make mistakes. Don't be too hard on yourself. It happens. Don't be discouraged. The important question you should be asking yourself is, *"What am I going to do about it now?"* I'm hoping your answer is, *"Get on the right track, starting today!"* This may be as easy as making a commitment to start paying your bills on time and to spend less. Or, it may require a little more work and focused attention. This depends on where you are today. Negative or "derogatory" items can stay on your report for up to seven years. Some negative items, such as bankruptcies and unpaid tax liens, can stay on your credit file for more than seven years and can affect your credit standing for a long time. Therefore, it's very important to get things paid down, paid up, and paid off—starting sooner rather than later.

- **Don't ignore it!** Start with looking at your three (one from each credit bureau) free credit reports. Remember, the best site for looking at all three of your credit reports is www.AnnualCreditReport. com. Check your credit reports to see what's being reported about you, what you owe, and who to contact.
- **Do you have collections or judgments on your credit report that are more than seven years old?** Federal law states that collections and judgments can impact your credit report for a maximum of *seven years*, and this is seven years after the initial delinquency date for collections and up to seven years from the file date for a judgment. It's not uncommon for collection agencies to sell your debt to another collection agency, which sometimes mistakenly resets the clock from a credit-reporting perspective and extends the seven-year period, but it should not. You, as a consumer, need to know that despite what is being reported (meaning, if there are any expired collections or judgments that are either paid or unpaid that are more than seven-years old on your credit files),

you should dispute these items and they should be deleted from your credit report without any problems. This does not necessarily mean the debt is forgiven. In some cases, it can still be pursued by the creditor or collection agency. The amount of time your debt is considered "collectible" varies from state-to-state. You can find details about "time barred debt" specific to your state by searching for this term on the Internet or by talking with a legal professional.

- **Dispute any incorrect or out-of-date information that appears on your report.** You can do this for free with the credit bureaus after ordering your credit reports on the www. AnnualCreditReport.com site. Erroneous and expired information may be negatively impacting your credit. Visit www.FTC.gov and search for "Disputing Errors on Credit Reports" for guidance.

- **Stick to the pay-back plan!** It may take you a while before you see the light at the end of the tunnel. Don't get discouraged. By showing them you are making an effort and taking the initiative, it demonstrates good faith on your part. This may prevent them from sending your account to a collection agency or taking legal action. It may also save you from paying additional fees and extra finance charges. Take ownership of your situation. That's what being an adult is about—owning your stuff! You've got to start somewhere and sometime, so why not start NOW? The sooner you begin, the sooner you will succeed!

- **If you're stuck in a credit crunch and feel like you need help, engage the assistance of a reputable credit counseling agency, such as the National Foundation for Credit Counseling (www. NFCC.org).** It may be worth a few minutes of your time to give them a call to see if they can assist you.

- **Beware of debt-settlement companies.** The promise of paying less than you owe may sound appealing to you, yet it's important to know that by doing this, it can cause additional harm to your credit standing. Talk to someone at the National Foundation for Credit Counseling (www.NFCC.org) first.

- **Beware of companies that claim they can easily and quickly fix your credit.** There is no magic fix with credit. The FTC (Federal Trade Commission) offers free information and warnings about credit repair. For more information, go to the FTC website (www.FTC.gov) and perform a search for "credit repair" in the site's search field. Educate yourself about credit repair – what is considered legitimate and what you can do yourself – before making any decisions to engage the assistance of a third-party that charges a fee.

- **Start doing all the right things with your open accounts!** We reviewed the right ways to achieve a good credit standing – by keeping your balances low and making regular, on-time payments. Follow these rules and apply these good credit-management practices to your open accounts and stick to them. If you don't have any open credit accounts in good standing, get one. Apply for a credit card, either a secured card or a regular card (which might be difficult if your credit is in bad shape). Use it once a month. Charge something small and pay the balance when you receive the bill. Do this for at least six to eight consecutive months to help improve your credit standing.
- **Credit can improve, so don't throw in the towel.** The necessary ingredients associated with improving your credit are *desire, knowledge, action, commitment, time and discipline.* You have all of them within yourself. It's up to you!

Destination: PRIME
Written by John Panzella

A week has passed. Aren't you proud?
Let everyone know. Shout it out loud!

A very strong start, wouldn't you say?
Six days down—plus one day!

Before you know it, a month will arrive
Another good reason for a deserved high-five!

In the blink of an eye, a year will go by,
It's true what they say, time really does fly.

Step-by-step, and one week at a time …
Are the pace and approach that will lead you to PRIME.

HELPFUL CREDIT-RELATED TERMS

This section contains several credit-related terms that can help with putting the pieces of the credit puzzle together. As I mentioned at the start of the book, I'm defining these items as I would explain them to my nephews with the basics of credit reporting in mind. Please take the time to read through them, because there's a helpful lesson associated with each term.

APR (Annual Percentage Rate) – This is the interest (finance charge) lenders, including credit card issuers, charge you for using their money. The higher the APR, the more interest you pay. To calculate the monthly interest rate on your balances, take the APR and divide by twelve to determine your monthly interest rate. For example, if your APR is eighteen percent, your monthly interest charge is 1.5% (eighteen divided by twelve is 1.5). This interest charge can be applied to your average daily balance or to your unpaid balance as of the billing statement closing date.

Some APRs are "fixed," meaning the stated APR will not change. Others are "variable," meaning they can change. Make sure you read the fine print and fully understand how your interest charges are calculated. Remember, paying your credit cards in full every month can help you avoid paying unnecessary finance charges.

AnnualCreditReport.com – The website you should use at least once every twelve months to obtain free copies of your credit reports. You are entitled to one free credit report from each of the three major credit bureaus every twelve months. You may also dispute inaccurate information on your credit report(s) directly with the credit bureaus.

Annual fee – Extra money above and beyond the balance that's owed to financial institutions, paid once per year.

Asset – An item of value, such as a home, car or money in the bank.

Balance – The total outstanding amount owed on a credit card or loan. The unpaid portion.

Bankruptcy – The legal status of a person (or an organization) unable to repay debts. A bankruptcy is considered a serious delinquency that can have a major negative impact to someone's credit standing.

Borrow (as in "borrowing" money) – The act of lending or receiving money with the intention of repayment.

Collateral – An asset, such as property or an automobile, that is pledged or used as security for the repayment of a loan that can be taken back (or repossessed) by the lender in the event of a missed payments.

Collection – An amount that's rightfully owed to a third-party (such as a lender, creditor) that has not been paid, has often gone several billing cycles beyond the due date and is now considered uncollectable. Usually, several efforts have been made by the party owed the money to collect the amount before it becomes categorized and noted on a credit report as a collection. A collection is a serious delinquency and can have a negative impact on your credit standing and credit scores.

Credit – The extension of money that allows a consumer to acquire the goods or services now with the expectation the money will be paid back, as agreed, over time.

Credit Limit – This is the maximum you can charge with a credit card— the ceiling.

Credit utilization ratio – This is the percentage of your balance as it relates to your credit limit. For example, if you have a **$250** balance on your open credit card and your credit limit is **$1000**, you are at a **twenty-five percent** credit-utilization ratio. The lower the credit utilization ratio, the better it will reflect on your credit standing. Remember, this factor applies to each individual open credit card as well as to your total balances in relation to your total available credit limits on all your open credit cards. Be cautious when closing credit cards, as this can eliminate some of your available credit limit, which can increase your total credit utilization ratio.

Creditor – A financial institution that extends credit to consumers.

Debt – Money you owe.

Default – A failure to pay what is legally owed.

Dispute – To challenge an item on your credit report by claiming it's inaccurate or outdated. You can do this at no cost directly with the credit bureaus. You can also dispute information directly with the company reporting the incorrect information to the credit bureau(s). I suggest doing both when possible.

Down Payment – Money that's required in advance of payments being made. Some loans require a down payment. Down payments are usually applied to the total balance, which reduces the amount financed. For example, if you were required to make a 20% down payment on a $20,000 car, this means you must pay $4,000 up front. This is the down payment. The difference (in this case, $16,000) is the amount financed.

Equity – The difference between the amount owed on the property (the mortgage) and the appraised value of the property. For example, a property is valued at $200,000 and the mortgage (the loan amount) is $120,000. The difference is $80,000, which represents the "equity" in the home. A "home equity" loan is a loan that leverages the equity of a home. In this case, it would be the $80,000. This is considered a "secured" loan (secured by the home's equity) and is often called a "second mortgage" or "home equity" loan in the lending industry.

Fees – Extra money that's owed to financial intuitions above and beyond what is borrowed, such as costs associated with originating loans or credit card processing fees.

Foreclosure/Short Sale – When a financial institution reclaims ownership of a home because of a home loan (a mortgage) not being paid as agreed.

Installment loan – A loan with a balance that is paid down every month with set payments. Examples of installment loans are auto loans and student loans. Credit cards are not considered installment loans. Credit cards are considered "revolving" debt.

Interest rate – See "APR."

Inquiry – (Also called a "credit inquiry") When someone reviews your credit report, they are "inquiring" about your credit status. This appears as an "inquiry" on your credit report. You have a right to know who has looked at your credit report. There are two credit inquiry types:

- **Soft inquiry** – A credit inquiry that does not impact your credit standing.
- **Hard inquiry** – A credit inquiry that can have an impact to your credit standing.

Judgment – A court order to pay a certain amount of money to a party (person or company) for damages resulting from a legal claim or lawsuit filed against you.

Lender – A financial institution that lends money to consumers.

Lending (as in "lending" money) – The act of extending money (or credit) with the intention of being paid back.

"Living BELOW your means" – A term that describes a financial lifestyle where someone spends less than what they earn. This lifestyle supports controlling spending and saving money. *"More cash. Less flash."*

"Living BEYOND your means" – A term that describes a financial lifestyle where someone spends more than what is earned by using loans and credit cards to support an unrealistic lifestyle. *"More flash. Less cash." This lifestyle tends to get people into a great deal of financial trouble.*

Minimum due – The minimum payment required (by the due date) to keep your account in good standing, usually expressed as a very small fraction of the total balance.

Paying a late fee – An unnecessary cost that could be avoided if you make your payments on time.

Public Record – Items that can appear on a credit report that are also on file with local, county, state and/or Federal courts. Items that fall under the category of "public records" can include bankruptcies, lawsuit judgments, and tax liens. Evictions, repossessions and foreclosures also fall under this category. Public records are considered serious delinquencies when they appear on a credit report.

Receipt – Proof of payment. Always get a receipt when buying goods and when making credit card payments, or at least have access to cancelled checks or online statements that can prove you have paid. Receipts are especially important when you pay anything using cash. Organize and store all your receipts. Another thing about receipts: when making your final payments for utilities, cable or cell phone service, request a receipt indicating "paid in full" and keep it. This can be especially helpful if they claim you owe an additional unpaid balance which, if not addressed, can potentially result in a collection on your credit report.

Repossession – When a financial institution reclaims ownership of a vehicle when an auto loan is not paid as agreed. Repossessions can appear on your credit report and can hurt your credit standing. Repossessions can be "voluntary" or "involuntary." Both will reflect negatively on your credit file and harm your credit standing.

Revolving debt – This is where your balance can vary month-to-month, as can the required minimum payments. The more you charge, the higher your payments. An example of revolving debt is credit card debt. Revolving debt is considered the riskiest type of debt from a credit-risk perspective.

Score (also called "credit score") – A number that reflects your credit worthiness based on the information reported on your credit report. Score ranges (low to high) can vary. Remember, there are different scoring models in use by different companies, and not all credit scores are calculated the same way. A good credit report will always produce a good credit score regardless of the scoring model and score range. If you're new to credit, focus more on building a strong credit record by following the advice in this book rather than chasing your credit score. A good credit score will come with time and good credit-management practices.

Secured/Unsecured debt – *Secured debt* means there is something that is "secured" to the debt, such as a home, car, or a deposit made on a secured credit card. If the loan is not paid back according to the agreement, the item or money that is "secured" can be taken back. *Unsecured debt* is when there is not an item or money being held to "secure" the debt, such as traditional credit cards or student loans.

Security deposits – Used as collateral to help protect the financial institution in the event of non-payment or other damages. Not the same as a down payment. Security deposits are usually not applied to the loan amount and can be refunded.

Statement closing date (Billing statement closing date) - The last day of the billing period on a loan or credit card statement. Your account information such as payments and account balances, as of the statement closing date, is typically what gets reported to the credit bureaus and noted on your credit reports.

Tax lien (federal) – Money owed to the Internal Revenue Service (IRS) from a taxpayer who fails to pay the federal government the taxes for which he or she is responsible.

TEST YOUR CREDIT KNOWLEDGE

How confident do you feel about credit? Now that you've finished reading the book, take a few minutes to test your credit knowledge with this 21-question credit quiz. You'll find the correct answers on the page following the quiz.

1. **Which of the following service providers and finance companies use credit in their decision-making and qualification processes?**

    A) Credit card companies
    B) Insurance companies
    C) Cell phone companies
    D) Landlords and Property Management companies
    E) Auto finance companies
    F) Mortgage lenders
    G) Utility and Cable providers
    H) All of the above

2. **Which of the following actions help build and maintain a good credit report?**

    A) Make all loan and credit card payments on time
    B) Keep credit card balances low
    C) Avoid applying for multiple credit cards in a short period of time
    D) Pay items not typically on your credit report, such as cable, cell phone and utilities in your name
    E) All of the above

3. **The maximum you can charge on a credit card is called....**

    A) The balance
    B) The default amount
    C) The credit limit
    D) The payment history

4. **Which percentage represents a "good" credit utilization ratio on open credit card accounts?**

   A) 30% or lower
   B) 50% to 60%
   C) 90%
   D) 100%

5. **Which spending cards can help with building a credit report at the credit bureaus?**

   A) Prepaid cards
   B) Gift cards
   C) Secured credit cards
   D) Debit/ATM cards used as credit cards

6. **Which of the below does not appear on a typical credit report?**

   A) Education level
   B) Income
   C) Checking and saving account balances
   D) Marital status
   E) All of the above

7. **A consumer with a good credit report containing a good payment history and low credit card balances reflect that of a _____ risk consumer.**

   A) High
   B) Lower

8. **A lower-risk consumer will generally pay _____ interest rates than a higher-risk consumer.**

   A) Higher
   B) Lower

9. **On a $20,000, 5-year (60 month) auto loan, how much more could a borrower with poor credit pay in finance charges over a borrower with good credit?**

   A) $500
   B) $1,000
   C) $3,000
   D) More than $5,000

10. **How many credit scores does the average consumer with an established credit history have?**

    A) One
    B) Three
    C) Many

11. **A good credit report will always produce a good credit score.**

    A) True
    B) False

12. **The three main credit bureaus, Equifax, TransUnion and Experian, offer consumers loans and credit cards.**

    A) True
    B) False

13. **If one credit bureau contains information reported to them from a specific lender, then all credit bureaus would have the same information.**

    A) True
    B) False

14. **Which site provides consumers with their free credit report from all three primary credit bureaus once every 12 months?**

    A) FreeCreditEveryYear.com
    B) AnnualCreditReport.com
    C) CreditCreditCredit.com

15. **How important is it to check your credit at least once a year to make sure the information the credit bureaus have on record about you is accurate?**

    A) Not very important
    B) Extremely important

16. **Which inquiry type can have a negative impact to your credit standing?**

    A) Soft
    B) Hard
    C) Both

17. **Checking your own personal credit report will not have a negative impact to your credit standing or credit scores.**

    A) True
    B) False

18. **Your credit record is an important part of your overall financial profile as an adult. What are the other important components?**

    A) Education, Training and Professional Development
    B) Income and Assets
    C) Taxes and Judgments

19. **If something you rightfully and legally owe goes unpaid, this can result in a(n) _____ appearing on your credit report.**

    A) Inquiry
    B) Collection
    C) Duplicate

20. **Which of the following can help with building your credit history?**

    A) Secured credit cards
    B) Credit Builder Loans
    C) Getting your parents to co-sign on an auto loan
    D) Traditional credit cards
    E) Student credit cards
    F) All of the above

21. **How long does it take to build a good credit report?**

    A) It happens automatically on your 18th birthday. No action is required
    B) Typically, 6 to 8 months of active and regular use of credit
    C) At least 5 years of using credit on an occasional basis

The correct answers to the credit quiz are on the next page.

Test Your Credit Knowledge – Quiz Answers

1.	H	All of the above
2.	E	All of the above
3.	C	The credit limit
4.	A	30% or lower
5.	C	Secured Credit Cards
6.	E	All of the above
7.	B	Lower
8.	B	Lower
9.	D	More than $5,000
10.	C	Many*
11.	A	True
12.	B	False
13.	B	False
14.	B	AnnualCreditReport.com
15.	B	Extremely Important
16.	B	Hard
17.	A	True
18.	B	Income and Assets
19.	B	Collection
20.	F	All of the above
21.	B	Typically, 6 to 8 months of active and regular use of credit

*Note: Answer 10, Remember, there are three main credit bureaus, but there are multiple credit-scoring models, many of which offer several versions, variations and industry influences (auto, mortgage, installment loan, etc..)

THE 12-MONTH PLAN TO BUILDING GOOD CREDIT

The 12-Month Plan to Building Good Credit

The next several pages contain a general road map that can help with building a solid credit report. The plan will be presented in several different phases focusing on specific timeframes. You can assign dates to these timeframes to create a personal plan and add your personal progress for each phase.

There are many ways to approach building your credit, which are detailed in the book. This is one approach. It's an independent and inexpensive way to establish credit in your name.

Remember; don't wait until you need credit to start building your credit record. The more you can do prior to financing an automobile or real estate, the better it can help you qualify for preferred financing - saving you lots of money. If you are of legal age and have income, now may be a good time to start.

Good credit management is a skill that needs to be developed – and taken very seriously. It requires your focus and dedicated attention. Credit can be fragile. It's important to approach credit with discipline, patience, great care, and a firm commitment to succeed.

Approach your credit-building plan with the understanding that it takes time. As indicated earlier in the book, it can take approximately 6 to 8 months to build enough credit to generate some of the credit scores used in the lending marketplace.

Are you ready?

The 12-Month Plan to Building Good Credit

First 30 days

Goal: Research and Prep

Suggested Actions:

Visit www.AnnualCreditReport.com

What information, if any, do the credit bureaus have on file about you? Are there any reporting errors that need to be addressed before getting started? If so, you should dispute them. If needed, seek guidance and assistance from the FTC.gov or the CFPB.gov.

Open a checking and/or savings account with a bank or credit union

This can help strengthen your overall financial profile. You may want to consider using a debit card linked to your bank account for your day-to-day incidentals to help you with managing your daily spending, and use your (soon to be acquired) secured credit card for monthly subscription services and fixed monthly expenses such as your cell phone bill.

Research and apply for a secured credit card

Many companies offer secured credit cards. You can search for the term "Secured Credit Cards" on the Internet for a variety of offerings. You can also talk to local banks and credit unions. Compare offerings. You're looking for the following:

- Low fees
- Reporting your utilization and payments to all three credit bureaus
- Will the secured credit card eventually convert to a traditional card?
- If so, when?
- When can your initial deposit be returned?

Research Credit Builder Loans (optional)

If you do not have the funds to make the initial deposit needed to open a secured credit card, you may want to start with a Credit Builder Loan. When the Credit Builder Loan is satisfied and you receive the funds, you may want to consider a secured credit card. Or, you can choose to do both at the same time - a secured credit card and a credit builder loan.

The remainder of the recommended road map will focus on the "secured credit card only" approach.

Progress Notes:

_____

_____

_____

_____

_____

_____

_____

_____

_____

_____

_____

_____

_____

_____

_____

_____

_____

_____

_____

_____

_____

_____

_____

_____

_____

_____

_____

_____

_____

_____

_____

_____

_____

_____

_____

_____

The 12-Month Plan to Building Good Credit

Next 2 to 7 months

Goals: Monthly responsible credit utilization. Establishing a good payment history.

Suggested Actions:

It's exciting to receive your very first credit card with your name on it. However, don't be too overzealous. Go slow. You may want to start with linking your monthly movie or music streaming subscription services, your cell phone and maybe other expenses that are recurring. Then, put your secured credit card away and use your debit card for your day-to-day purchases.

You will receive a monthly bill showing the charges applied to your credit card. Pay the bill on time every month. You can write a check and mail it to the credit card company, or visit a local bank branch to pay your bill. Or, link your credit card account to your checking or savings account, and then transfer the funds on-line (if this option is made available to you).

Active and regular (monthly) use of credit is essential to building your credit. Remember; be mindful of your credit utilization ratio. The lower the balance in relation to the credit limit, the better this will reflect. Strive for a 30% or lower credit utilization ratio when using your credit cards. Remember, your credit card balance, as of the statement closing date, is reported to the credit bureaus and is used to calculate your credit utilization ratio.

Progress Notes:

_____

_____

_____

_____

_____

_____

_____

_____

_____

_____

_____

_____

_____

_____

_____

_____

_____

_____

_____

_____

_____

_____

_____

_____

_____

_____

_____

_____

_____

_____

_____

The 12-Month Plan to Building Good Credit

8th Month

Goals: Continued responsible monthly credit utilization. Continue building a good payment history. Expand your credit relationships (optional).

Suggested Actions:

Now that you have several months of credit history on record, you will have more options. And as long as you've managed your credit responsibly over the last several months, you should have a good credit history and an established credit score across all credit scoring models.

Talk to the secured credit card issuer about converting your card to a "traditional" credit card. If they can do this for you, ask about getting your initial deposit returned.

If they do not offer a conversion option, you may want to consider shopping around for a traditional credit card that meets your needs. At this stage, you should consider a major credit card that offers you free credit scores every month with your bill to help track your progress with building credit.

You may need to re-link your monthly auto-payment subscription services to your new credit card if a new account number is issued.

Continue to use credit monthly, be mindful of your payment due dates and credit utilization ratios.

Progress Notes:

The 12-Month Plan to Building Good Credit

Next 9 to 11 Months

Goals: Continued responsible monthly credit utilization. Continue building a good payment history.

Suggested Actions:

At this point, you should be on a strong path to achieving good credit. Keep it going! If you are receiving a free credit score every month with your monthly bill, you should see it continue to increase every month. If so, you're doing all the right things. However, if your credit score is falling, it's important to understand the reason it's headed in the opposite direction.

Are your balances higher than they have been?

Did you miss a payment due date?

Did you apply for any new credit cards recently?

Remember, hard inquiries associated with applying for new credit can have a temporary minor negative impact to your credit score. If you opened a new credit card account in the last month or two, the credit inquiry, combined with the lowering of the "average age" of your credit relationships, can negatively impact your score. If this is the case, don't stress too hard about it. As the hard inquiries age, they will have less of a negative impact. And your accounts will continue to mature, which will help improve your credit standing. In the meantime, keep doing the right things with your existing credit relationships – make your payments on time and keep your balances low.

Progress Notes:

_____

_____

_____

_____

_____

_____

_____

_____

_____

_____

_____

_____

_____

_____

_____

_____

_____

_____

_____

_____

_____

_____

_____

_____

_____

_____

_____

_____

_____

_____

_____

_____

_____

The 12-Month Plan to Building Good Credit

12 Months Later

Goals: Continued responsible monthly credit utilization. Continue building a good payment history. Check your credit reports.

Suggested Actions:

Happy Anniversary! At this stage, you should have a full year of successful credit management under your belt. You should have a good credit standing and a good credit score! Congratulations!

If you are receiving your credit score monthly with your credit card bill, you should be happy with the score and where you are in the credit score range, although you may think that you should fall higher in the scale. This is normal. Not to worry – you will achieve a higher score in time and with more experience and variety. At this stage, you should be in fairly good shape and ready for other types of credit relationships, such as an automobile loan. And the good news is you're not starting from scratch. Your credit score, at this stage, should qualify you for good financing terms, saving you some serious money. Pat yourself on the back!

Now that 12 months have passed, you are eligible to review your credit reports again using www.AnnualCreditReport.com at no charge. It's a good idea to do this every year to make sure the information the credit bureaus have on file about you is accurate.

There are other consumer-friendly, legitimate sites that offer free credit information and scores. Signing-up for these services will not negatively impact your credit standing or credit score. These services can provide you with general guidance and educational information about credit. Keep in mind the scoring models they offer may not be the same scoring model used by lenders or credit card companies, so don't get stuck on a credit score number. Rather, review where your credit score falls in the range, pay attention to the upward or downward trend your credit score is following, and stay on the path that will continue to build and strengthen your personal credit file.

Progress Notes:

_____

_____

_____

_____

_____

_____

_____

_____

_____

_____

_____

_____

_____

_____

_____

_____

_____

_____

_____

_____

_____

_____

_____

_____

_____

_____

_____

_____

_____

_____

_____

_____

HELPFUL CREDIT-RELATED RESOURCES

There's tons of information on the Internet about credit reporting, credit scoring, credit education, and consumer rights as they relate to credit and credit cards. Here are a few helpful websites and resources for your reference:

www.NFCC.org – National Foundation for Credit Counseling, a nonprofit credit-counseling agency. There's also a helpful "Consumer Tools" section, that includes calculators, a budget worksheet, consumer tips, and videos.

www.CFPB.gov – Consumer Financial Protection Bureau, a U.S. Government agency that assists consumers with problems and issues experienced with banks, lenders and other financial organizations.

www.AnnualCreditReport.com – This site allows you to request a free credit report once every twelve months from each of the national consumer credit-reporting agencies Equifax, Experian, and TransUnion.

www.OptOutPreScreen.com – This site allows consumers to "opt-in" or "opt-out" of offers of credit or insurance. In other words, if you choose to opt-out, you should no longer receive pre-approval offers and other forms of (what I call) "junk mail" in your mailbox.

www.CreditCards.com and **www.BankRate.com** - These sites provide information about credit card offers, rates, and other helpful information about credit cards and loans. They also offer tools, tips, and techniques related to credit that can be of assistance to consumers.

www.Experian.com, **www.Equifax.com,** **www.TransUnion. com** – Websites for the three main credit bureaus, Experian, Equifax and TransUnion.

www.consumer.ftc.gov/topics/money-credit – Good information about money and credit.

www.banking.senate.gov – Here is where you can find more information about the Credit CARD Act mentioned earlier in the book.

www.FTC.gov – Federal Trade Commission, consumer protection, consumer rights.

www.FTC.gov/IDTHEFT – Federal Trade Commission. Free information, including publications, covering all aspects of Identity Theft

www.IdentityTheft.gov – A site to report identity theft and get a personal recovery plan

www.JohnKnowsCredit.com – The author's website. Also on Facebook under "John Knows Credit"

AUTHOR'S FINAL THOUGHTS

My hope is that the information contained in this book can help with giving you a strong beginning as you navigate your way through a world in which credit plays a significant part. As mentioned earlier in the book, I wish I knew and understood information about credit when I was a young adult.

Credit is so important—and yet can be so fragile. Every time you use credit, you are putting yourself at risk. Treat your credit with great care and responsibility, and you'll find that it will pay you dividends over your lifetime. Remember, your credit standing reflects your financial character, reliability, and reputation and should be taken very seriously.

Building good credit is much like climbing a mountain. It may take a while to reach the top, but with time, patience, discipline, and the right tools (in this case, knowledge), you will reach the top where you can enjoy the view. However, without the proper tools, it's easy to slip. And, as is the case with climbing a mountain, the fall can be faster than the climb. But not to worry, the mountain will always be there, and so will the view from the top. Try not to get discouraged, and keep climbing!

Thank you for taking the time to read *Give Yourself Some Credit*. I truly hope it has and will continue to help you build a long and successful relationship with your credit. Oh, and before I forget, I'm always interested in your feedback. You can reach me at JohnKnowsCredit@gmail.com. I'm on Facebook under "John Knows Credit," and my website is www. JohnKnowsCredit.com.

Thank you, and *Give Yourself Some Credit* for taking the time to learn about credit!

All is well.
John

ABOUT THE AUTHOR

John Panzella is a multi-certified credit expert. He is a skilled and experienced presenter and educator on the topics of credit reporting and credit scoring. Since 2009, John has conducted hundreds of credit-education seminars across the country. His expertise includes the Fair Credit Reporting Act (FCRA) credit-reporting guidelines, evaluating credit reports, providing guidance on how to improve personal credit standing, and assessing damaging actions that can impact credit and credit scores. John is FCRA certified by the Consumer Data Industry Association, the trade association of the credit reporting agencies. He has more than twenty-five years of experience working in the financial-services industry, including seventeen years in the credit reporting industry. John can be reached at JohnKnowsCredit@gmail.com.

CPSIA information can be obtained
at www.ICGtesting.com
Printed in the USA
FFOW03n1715010518
46431119-48284FF